UPRISING

HOW TO
BUILD A BRAND
—AND CHANGE THE WORLD—

BY SPARKING
CULTURAL MOVEMENTS

scott goodson

New York   Chicago   San Francisco   Lisbon   London
Madrid   Mexico City   Milan   New Delhi
San Juan   Seoul   Singapore   Sydney   Toronto

1 2 3 4 5 6 7 8 9 0   DOC/DOC   1 6 5 4 3 2

ISBN   978-0-07-178282-1
MHID   0-07-178282-6

e-ISBN   978-0-07-178281-4
e-MHID   0-07-178281-8

This publication is designed to provide accurate and authoritative information in regard to the subject matter covered. It is sold with the understanding that neither the author nor the publisher is engaged in rendering legal, accounting, securities trading, or other professional service. If legal advice or other expert assistance is required, the services of a competent professional person should be sought.

> —*From a Declaration of Principles Jointly Adopted*
> *by a Committee of the American Bar Association*
> *and a Committee of Publishers and Associations*

McGraw-Hill books are available at special quantity discounts to use as premiums and sales promotions or for use in corporate training programs. To contact a representative, please e-mail us at bulksales@mcgraw-hill.com.

This book is printed on acid-free paper.

Library of Congress Cataloging-in-Publication Data
Goodson, Scott.
  Uprising : how to build a brand—and change the world—by sparking cultural movements / by Scott Goodson.
       p. cm.
  Includes bibliographical references and index.
  ISBN 978-0-07-178282-1 (alk. paper) — ISBN 0-07-178282-6 (alk. paper)
  1. Branding (Marketing) 2. Social movements. I. Title.
  HF5415.1255.G673 2012
  658.8'02—dc23
                                                          2011048789

CONTENTS

Preface

As I was finishing the writing of this book, in the summer and early fall of 2011, just as we were launching a marketing movement called "Rise" for Mahindra, one of India's most powerful companies, it seemed that uprisings and movements were happening everywhere around the planet. Egypt had fallen. Libyans had overthrown a powerful leader in Muammar Qaddafi and there continued to be mounting resistance against Bashar al-Assad in Syria. Europe's economic turmoil had sparked demonstrations and sometimes riots in England, Spain, and Greece. Protests targeting government corruption were occurring in India, led by one man who ignited a movement that changed government. Israelis had taken to the streets to rail against the rising costs of housing. In Canada, we saw that one foolish remark could spark a movement: after a Toronto policeman declared that women should stop dressing like "sluts" to avoid being assaulted, there were large rallies (first in Canada, then in other countries) in which women purposely dressed provocatively as part of the protest.

And then there was the movement that erupted within shouting distance of StrawberryFrog's office in lower Manhattan. When the Occupy Wall Street (OWS) protesters first began to assemble, it seemed like a small and not-all-that-impressive version of the larger Twitter-fueled protest movements that had sprung up elsewhere around the world. I recall that the mainstream media coverage of OWS had a derisive tone early on; the suggestion was that this ragtag bunch of protesters didn't really know what they wanted, and that they'd probably drift away after a couple of days.

That didn't happen, as we all know. Instead, the "Occupy" movement persisted and soon provoked a police overreaction; this in turn fueled the fire of the movement and attracted more people. The tone of the media coverage changed—this was no longer something that could be easily dismissed. Then the movement spread to other cities, and other countries.

Yet at its core, it remained small. As I visited Zuccotti Park at various stages of the OWS movement, I was struck by the fact that it seemed pretty much the same before and after it became world famous: Through it all, the heart of the movement continued to be just a modest group of people gathered in a downtown New York park. And yet it had somehow managed to become something that all of us, everywhere, were paying attention to, thinking about, engaging with, and arguing about. Even my two young sons—Jacoby, age 9, and Ellis, age 7—were talking about it one day with their mother Karin over dinner. Meanwhile, *Time* magazine named "The Protester" as its Person of the Year for 2011.

This is the power of movements: They can start out with just a small group of people who believe passionately in something. And they can end up changing the culture . . . around the world.

Having studied movements for the better part of two decades, I can tell you that the OWS movement has reinforced and confirmed much of what I've learned about movements over the years, and much of what is shared in the pages ahead. Specifically, it stands as the most current proof that:

- Movements tend to form around a compelling "idea on the rise" (in this case, the idea being that the "99 percent" who aren't in the top 1 percent income bracket have been getting royally shafted of late, and need to make some noise about it)

- Movements today can spread like wildfire because of communications technology and social media

- Even though a movement can spread digitally, it still needs to have a physical-world presence—in the park, in the town square, or on the streets

- There's nothing like a "provocation" (e.g., an overreaction involving pepper spray) to give a movement traction

- Once a movement gets started, it can be very hard to predict or control where it will go, how it will evolve or change, when it will end, or what it will ultimately achieve

Whether OWS will ultimately have an impact on the issue of income inequality or reinvent America is hard to say. But one thing it has already achieved is to awaken people to the power of movements. I believe many who've watched what transpired in Zuccotti Park can't help wondering, *How can I be part of something like that?* Or, *Could I possibly help start something like that, based around an issue or an idea that matters deeply to me?*

Among those asking this question will be activists, educators, politicians, community leaders, tech innovators, artists, concerned citizens—and business people.

That last group may seem out of place at the march. What does business have to do with movements? Aren't movements such as OWS *against* business? Aren't movements supposed to be about noble causes and higher purposes—as opposed to selling stuff?

Those are great questions that I'll tackle in the book. I expect that when I'm done, some will still feel that business has no business getting involved with movements.

But here's what I think. Movements—at least, the kind of movements that gather around positive, creative, dynamic ideas—can help build a better, fairer, more sustainable, and more interesting world. They can help individuals to rally support for worthy causes; help an innovator build momentum behind a new idea; they can even put someone in the White House. From a business standpoint, they can enable a company to form a stronger connection to the public. And yes, that certainly can translate into profit, though I think it can also have other effects that are less mercenary but no less important.

As businesses become involved with the right kinds of movements—and if they do so in an authentic manner that supports and facilitates, rather than tries to exploit—I believe this can help companies themselves to attain a higher sense of purpose. It can allow them to associate with and support worthwhile endeavors. And it can bring the world of business closer to people and their everyday concerns, passions, and goals. It can also, by the way, be a hell of a lot of fun—because there's nothing quite like a good uprising to get the blood circulating.

Acknowledgments

Creating this book was like launching a movement. I needed a lot of help and support from many true believers and I'd like to thank them all. Let me start by thanking two people who helped greatly with the research and writing. Laura O'Connor conducted many interviews and gathered mountains of research for the book. Warren Berger, a gifted writer and a friend, helped tremendously with the overall organization and the writing of the book. And many people at the StrawberryFrog agency in New York, Amsterdam, and São Paulo contributed their insights and energy to the project, in particular Kevin McKeon, Ole Pedersen, Heather LeFevre, Peralta, Patricia DeLuca, Corinna Falusi, Danielle Simon, Aleks Bookman, Chip Walker, Will Allen, Jake Baldridge, David Orton, and Tiffany Tagle.

I also want to thank the clients who allowed us to share their stories in the book: Anand Mahindra, Kevin George, Chris Bauder, and Rob Mason at Jim Beam; Kipp Kreutzberg; Smart Car's Kim McGill; Pepsico's True North brand; the former Pepsi marketing chief, Jill Beraud; Jaya Kumar; P&G's Daniel Epstein, Patrick Kraus,

Andy Daly; Sabra's Ken Kunze, Ronen Zohar, and Mina Penna; and Mahindra's Dr. Pawan Goenka, Ruzbeh Irani, Karthik Balakrishnan, Rajesh Jejurikar, Pravin Shah, Anoop Mathur, and Sheetal Meta.

I relied on various experts to help me get a better understanding of the dynamics of movements, both in the business world and in the social realm. Starting with business, Guy Kawasaki offered great insights on Apple, Lee Clow of TBWA gave us the inside story on movements launched for Pedigree and other brands, and Dominik Imseng shared a deep knowledge of VW's "Think Small" movement. Bob Johansen of the Institute for the Future offered his crystal ball view of how movements are likely to affect business in the years ahead. Mark McKinnon gave us the inside scoop on political movements. Timo Lumme of the International Olympic Committee gave us wonderful insights into the Olympic movement. And George Hirthler was always there as a friend.

Several top psychology/sociology experts shared insights, including Saskia Sassen of Columbia University and Dr. Kathleen Gershen at New York University. The author Daniel Pink (*Drive*) helped me understand what "drives" people to join movements. I was inspired by many books and articles that deal with how movements form and how technology is changing group dynamics. In particular I want to cite the work of Neil Smelser, a pioneer in the study of social movements. Also, Mark Earls (*Herd*), Clay Shirky (*Here Comes Everybody* and *Cognitive Surplus*), Douglas Atkin (*The Culting of Brands*), Seth Godin (*Tribes*), and Sally Hogshead (*Fascinate*). And I want to cite the fascinating research on "swarm theory" produced by Princeton University Professor Ian Cousins. Thanks also to Adam Morgan (*Eating the Big Fish*) for both sharing insights and connecting me to other sources.

A special thanks goes out to all the people who shared their stories of launching movements. This includes Rob Walden and Lois Steinberg of the The Age in Place movement; Ned Dodington and Matthew Wettergreen of Caroline Collective; Faythe Levine of Handmade Nation; Blake Mycoskie of TOMS Shoes; Jason Kibbey, CEO of PACT; Angela Daffon of Jodi's Voice; Erik Proulx of Lemonade; Jeremy Heimens, CEO and founder of Purpose.com; and Navid Ghani, professor of sociology.

I also want to mention two people who believed in this book from the start and helped bring it to life: my literary agent, Jud Laghi, and the original editor of the book, Niki Papadopoulos, as well as Donya Dickerson and Pattie Amoroso of McGraw-Hill.

Thanks also to my good friends Allan and Bella Gordon, Richard and Irene Gossett, Pauline and Marshall Brown, John and Suzanne Davis, Margareta Kull, Warren Cable, Linda and Scott Samios, Kal and Jeff Drummond, Anthony Kalamut, Katy and Tom Cowe, and Louis LaFlamme, who were rock solid there for me.

Last, I want to close by thanking my wife, Karin, and my two sons, Jacoby and Ellis, who believed in me and this project, and breathed life into a vision that had been a whisper and a dream in my head, and gave me unlimited love and support. I want to thank my family, Anna and Sylvie, Joelly and Perry, Tracy and Maxx, Leslie, Carl Adam Drakenberg, Ulla, and John, and my mother, Sylvia, for being there when I needed it and for their support. Thanks, Dad, for the inspiration.

Here's to all the passionate souls out there who are sparking movements big and small and making a difference in the world.

Scott Goodson
November 2011

CHAPTER 1

What Is a Movement?

AND WHY SHOULD IT MATTER TO YOUR COMPANY?

It began with a couple of celebrity deaths: first the soul singer Barry White, then the comic actor John Ritter. Both died of heart attacks, and in each case, the death led to the predictable media cycle of nostalgic film clips and fond farewells. That should have been the end of it, but it wasn't.

In the weeks that followed, friends and relatives of White and Ritter began to make high-profile public appearances, talking about something called *CVD*. The letters stood for cardiovascular disease, but in much of the ensuing public discussion, which circulated through the broadcast media, on the Internet, and gradually on the street, only the acronym was used, stirring intrigue among those who began to tune in to this rising chatter. What was this CVD? And why did people seem to be so agitated about it?

Those who joined the growing grassroots conversation—and hundreds of thousands did, in the spring and summer of 2004—learned that CVD was killing people faster than guns, cancer, and AIDS combined, and that this enemy was wreaking particular havoc on the baby-boom generation. Therefore, it was up to the boomers to confront this scourge—by coming together and fighting the good fight, just as they did back in the 1960s. Seemingly overnight, a movement with its own manifesto sprang into existence. There were T-shirts, impromptu rallies, and organized concerts. There was a website with a million hits. And while the movement had no apparent leader, it did have a name: the Boomer Coalition.

The Boomer Coalition became front-page news for a time, attracted celebrities, and spread like wildfire before, inevitably, it gradually started to lose momentum. But along the way, it managed to achieve what any cultural movement worth the name strives to do: it brought about change. In this case, change took the form of dramatically heightened public awareness of the risks of cardiovascular diseases and the steps that can be taken to minimize that risk. The Boomer Coalition shifted the cultural dialogue in a way that persisted long after the rallies were over and the T-shirts were gone.

When popular movements or uprisings such as the Boomer Coalition occur—and they are occurring more and more frequently in today's tech-empowered, social-networked society—the root sources of the movement can be the subject of considerable scholarly debate. What were the societal conditions and pressures that set the stage for this groundswell? Who or what lit the first spark? And when did it all reach the Gladwellian tipping point?

The answers are usually complicated, unclear, and subject to interpretation. However, this isn't true in the case of The Boomer Coalition. If you want to know what lit that spark, the answer is simple: I did.

This was in the early days of my marketing agency named StrawberryFrog, and at the time one of my clients was a maverick marketer named Kipp Kreutzberg at the large pharmaceutical company Pfizer. Pfizer had a number of drugs on the market related to cardiovascular health, and the company needed to do something innovative to wake up baby boomers to the risk of heart attacks. It could have taken the usual course: run commercials about heart disease that most people would tune out. Instead, I suggested that it carefully build, from the ground up, a movement based around the theme of boomers fighting heart disease.

The plan was to approach a few high-profile people who'd been affected by the issue (starting with the relatives of White and Ritter) to help get the public conversation started, then create platforms where people could come together to focus on this cause, including a website, rock concerts, viral films, and street events— anything and everything that could foster the groundswell. My agency had done this type of initiative for a number of other clients with very successful results, but Pfizer, a pretty conservative company by nature, was nervous about some of it. The plan required that the company keep its own name out of the spotlight, at least in the early stages. It also required that it ditch the rules of advertising and give up control of the message to the public. And after sparking the movement, Pfizer would have to just stand back and see what might happen.

What happened was a highly successful awareness campaign that engaged millions of boomers, doctors, and pharma employees. It surprised Pfizer, but not StrawberryFrog; we'd seen this strategy work for companies ranging from shoemakers to car manufacturers, from retailers and banks to cable television networks. This is why, over the past decade, we've become convinced that "movement marketing" is the new way forward for anyone who is trying to sell products, earn customer loyalty, influence public opinion, solve social problems, and, quite possibly, change the world.

WHAT DO MOVEMENTS HAVE TO DO WITH BUSINESS?

Throughout history, popular movements have given us many of our cherished freedoms, our finest heroes, and our basic human rights—so what do they have to do with the crass and superficial business of selling stuff? And what makes anyone think that he or she can plan and calculate something as spontaneous and authentic as a movement? And lastly, what makes movements so important at this particular moment in time?

To begin with the last question, while it's true that people have been starting movements for a very long time, a profound change is underway right now. It is easier than ever before for people to band together around a shared idea, goal, or passion—and they are doing so every day. As we'll see in this book, people are coming together to rebuild communities, rescue animals, reinvent the political process, get rid of front lawns, introduce new ways of teaching kids, create new housing for seniors, go barefoot, go naked, dress up as eighteenth-century figures—these days, if you can think of a cause or a passion or even just a pastime, chances are you'll find a group of people who care enough about it to have formed a movement (see Figure 1-1).

The current movement mania is being fueled by several factors, the most obvious one being technology. The Internet, and in particular the rise of social media, has made it easy to find and connect with like-minded souls. And that same technology makes it possible for a group, once formed, to organize, plan, and take action.

But there are other social factors at work, too: while people today are more connected in one sense, they're also more disconnected—from their neighbors and from some of the traditional community gatherings of yesteryear (from the Elks Club to Tupperware parties) that used to provide social hubs. Movements are becoming the new gathering points.

FOR EVERY PASSION	THERE IS A MOVEMENT
Making jewelry	Etsy movement
Saving at-risk pets	ARM (animal rescue movement)
Victorian style + gadgets	Steam-punk movement
The pursuit of happiness	The Happiness Project
Upholding the Constitution	Tea Party movement
Independence in old age	Aging-in-place movement
Doing good deeds, easily	Pepsi Refresh Project
Being one's own boss	Free Agent Nation
Improving lives of poor kids	Tom's Shoes
Low-impact transportation	Slow Bicycle movement
Collaborative problem solving	InnoCentive movement
Harmless pranks	"ImprovEverywhere" movement
Communes	Co-housing movement

Figure 1-1

At the same time, movements are offering a means of finding reassurance and purpose in a world that has become increasingly unsettling. "In times of turbulence, anything that gives people a sense of meaning tends to grow," says Bob Johansen, one of the directors of the Institute for the Future think tank. "Movements have a strong meaning component to them—it's what attracts people to them in the first place. And so as the world gets more and more volatile and complicated in the years ahead, we can expect movements to become increasingly important."

YOU DON'T HAVE TO OVERTHROW A GOVERNMENT TO BE PART OF A MOVEMENT

We all have some sense of what a movement is. However, many people may associate that word with big, world-changing social phenomena: the women's suffrage movement or the civil rights movement. Along with these important social movements, there have been groundbreaking cultural movements that tend to be associated with the arts and ways of thinking, such as the Renaissance or, more narrowly, Italian Neorealism. Then, too, many great religions grew and spread as movements. And today, throughout the Middle East and beyond, we see a wave of independence movements that are shaking and sometimes breaking the existing geopolitical foundations.

All of the movements just mentioned can be thought of as "movements with a capital M," because what we're talking about in these cases is truly important, history-making stuff. And there's definitely a place for some discussion of these capital-M movements in the pages ahead; there are fascinating dynamics in and lessons to be learned from everything from the uprising in Egypt to the current Tea Party and Occupy Wall Street movements in the United States.

But through much of the book, you'll find a focus on movements that may seem more modest in scope and of far less historical significance. These "movements with a small m" may involve, say, a group of passionate activists, creative types, or even rabid consumers of a particular product. When these people band together around a shared passion or idea and try to turn it into something bigger and more significant, they're not necessarily trying to change history or to change the world as we know it. They're just trying to change the world (or some small part of it) as *they* know it.

MOVEMENT PROMOTING KINDNESS

EXEMPLAR DO ONE NICE THING

THE BIG IDEA Doing at least one nice thing per week makes the world a better place. Debbie Tenzer started this regimen as a way to combat the "Monday Blues" and found that doing good for others was more rewarding than she expected. So she started a website and e-mails different assignments to her followers, who follow through with charitable acts. Tenzer calls her members "nice-o-holics."

STARTED Debbie Tenzer founded Do One Nice Thing in Los Angeles in June 2005.

HOW IT SPREAD Do One Nice Thing's monthly e-mails reminding people to act ask people to spread the message. Media coverage has included extensive radio appearances on broadcasts like Oprah's and Martha Stewart's, newspaper and magazine coverage, and extensive blog mentions. Tenzer created kits for members to start their own local clubs. Her 2009 book titled *Do One Nice Thing*, including Tenzer's top 100 favorite nice things along with tips, became a self-help bestseller, popular with book clubs.

WHERE IT STANDS NOW   Do One Nice Thing has members in more than 92 countries. More than 100 tons of school supplies have been sent to U.S. soldiers for children in Iraq and Afghanistan; tens of thousands of books have been given to schools, libraries, and children's hospitals; and tens of thousands of cans of food and other items have been donated to food banks.

QUOTE   "Maybe I can't solve our big problems, but I know I can do something."—Debbie Tenzer

WEBSITE   DoOneNiceThing.com

If you break it down to a four-point quadrant, movements can range from small to big, and from personal to societal (see Figure 1-2).

The upper right-hand quadrant of this chart (large/societal) would include everything from the civil rights movement in the 1960s to the Middle East today. But quite a few of the movements you'll read about in this book started out in the lower left quadrant (small/personal). And I think they represent something quite interesting, particularly from the standpoint of marketers or anybody else who is trying to exert cultural influence, because while the really earthshaking social movements in the upper right quadrant are probably too big, too volatile, and ultimately too important to even think about in marketing terms, those smaller,

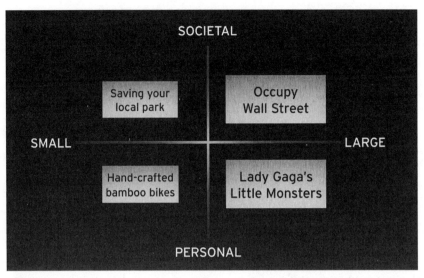

Figure 1-2

everyday movements are more accessible and sometimes in need of jump-starting or nurturing. There are countless opportunities for companies to connect with these movements with a small m— or possibly even to launch a modest movement of their own.

PASSION: THE ONLY PREREQUISITE

The point is that it isn't necessary for something to be earthshaking to qualify as a movement. It can be a phenomenon that affects a limited group of people. And it doesn't have to be righteous or profound—it could involve relatively mundane matters like what people are eating or whether they're choosing to live in communes. And although I'll be using the term *cultural movements* throughout the book, this doesn't mean that a movement has to be about high culture or art. What I'm talking about are the shared behaviors, attitudes, styles, influences, and beliefs that surround us—the "culture" we're living in at this moment in time. Art is part of that culture, of course, but so are a million other, less lofty things, from what we're watching on TV to what we're obsessing about on Twitter at any given time. The culture we live in is subject to constant change, and one big agent of that change is movements. When they're successful, movements tend to shift the dialogue and add something new and dynamic to the cultural ecosystem that we all share.

There are hundreds, perhaps thousands, of movements small and large happening all around us. As far as I'm aware, there are no available statistics tracking the actual growth in the number of movements, but it's clear that this phenomenon has exploded in the past few years. In the pages ahead, we'll see examples that range far and wide: movements about people expressing their creativity through craftwork, joining together to take on a problem (such as cancer or crime), or finding new ways to live together (the co-housing movement) or work together (the co-working movement).

MOVEMENT THE DIY LIFESTYLE

EXEMPLAR   MAKER FAIRE

THE BIG IDEA   "All of us are makers." The Maker Faire is a roaming festival, featuring art, technology, crafts, and science, where like-minded folks gather to celebrate the do-it-yourself creative mindset.

STARTED   Dale Dougherty, of *MAKE* magazine from O'Reilly Media, founded it in California in April 2006.

HOW IT SPREAD   The Maker Faire is supported by *MAKE* magazine, makezine.com, craftzine.com, and O'Reilly Media, all of whose customers are the kind of early adopters that make for a robust online community. The faires also have a number of corporate sponsors spreading the word, such as Radio Shack, Microsoft, Autodesk, and Etsy.

WHERE IT STANDS NOW   The Maker Faire just celebrated its sixth annual Bay Area event with some 100,000 people in attendance. It has traveled to Kansas City, Detroit, and New York City, and has spawned a host of community-produced mini-Maker Faires in places as far-flung as Brighton, U.K., and Vancouver. A fall 2011 World Maker Faire in New York City had more than 500 exhibitors, with a special emphasis on innovations in health care. More than 16,000 people follow the Maker Faire on Facebook, and the movement has inspired imitator faires in Africa.

QUOTE   "It's important to understand that a lot of the origins of our industries come from this idea of playing and figuring things out in groups."—Dale Dougherty

WEBSITE   MakerFaire.com

The growth of movements has been fueled by new technology that makes it easier for members of a movement to find one another and coordinate their activities. But the role of technology in movements (which we'll examine more closely in Chapter 4) is secondary to what really drives the growth and success of any movement: passion. Whether a movement is large or small, or whether its central idea is profound or playful, for a movement to actually take wing, people must feel strongly enough about something to want to take some type of collective action—to actually *move* on that idea together, usually with the goal of bringing about some level of change.

In his book *Tribes*, the author and marketing guru Seth Godin describes a movement as "an idea that spreads with passion through a community." While I don't necessarily think Godin's word *tribe* is quite right for describing the people who belong to movements (in many ways movements are not tribal at all, because they actually tend to be heterogeneous, democratically run, and open to anyone who wants to join), I do think Godin has hit the nail on the head when it comes to the importance of passion. It is passion that transforms an idea into a movement. It's what makes people want to talk about and share that particular idea. What's more, it inspires people to want to expend tremendous amounts of energy, often without compensation, on behalf of the cause.

Passion enables movements to grow and, ultimately, to have a significant impact on the culture. We're seeing now that movements that begin humbly at a grassroots level can have ramifications that extend to the highest levels of power. For example, politicians seeking office nowadays increasingly need to spark movements, or to find a way to align with existing ones, in order to be elected. In American politics, movement mania—starting with the 2008 popular surge that carried Barack Obama to the presidency, and continuing with the subsequent Tea Party movement that sprang up in opposition to some of Obama's policies and positions—is already firmly entrenched.

Meanwhile, community leaders seeking to implement new programs may need the strength and passion of movements to get traction and bring about change. Nonprofits, education reformers, indie rock bands, and innovators of almost any kind are apt to find that new ideas and approaches have a much better chance of becoming reality if they're carried on the shoulders of some kind of popular movement. Basically, anyone whose objective is to persuade people to do something must now begin to come to terms with an emerging truth: persuading the individual is often best achieved by influencing the group that surrounds the individual.

A NEW BUSINESS MODEL: "MOVEMENT MARKETING"

This fundamental shift will have—indeed, is already having—particular impact on the world of business. For the better part of a century, business has relied on a marketing model focused on persuading individuals to buy products or services. But the dirty little secret (which is not so secret anymore) is that all those expensive plugs for "new and improved" offerings are falling upon deaf ears. No one's listening to you, especially if you're talking about your product.

But we *are* listening to one another, and we do care about lots of things (other than your product): cleaning up the environment, reinventing ourselves, underground rock, solving social problems, scrapbooking, eating healthy, and countless other passions that are forming the basis of movements small and large. The best chance for today's would-be persuaders is to ditch the sales pitch and start trying to figure out what people care about and how to be part of that conversation.

Right now, some of the most established companies in the world (Procter & Gamble and PepsiCo among them) are starting to come to terms with this change. This is why those companies, in spite of their size and their longtime investment in the convention-al 30-second TV spot marketing model, have now begun to make the transition to movement marketing. They are recognizing that in the "postproduct era" of today and tomorrow, the smartest marketing will not be about "whiter whites" or "rack-and-pinion steering." It will be about connecting with society on ideas and issues that actually matter to people. And in trying to achieve that aim, *the movement will be the medium*, serving as the ideal channel to carry and spread a message that is authentic and compelling.

The challenge for these companies—or for entrepreneurs, politicians, and change makers of all types who want to tap into the growing power of movements—is figuring out how to align themselves with existing movements or, better yet, how to spark new ones. Having studied and tried to influence movements for years, I can attest that it is a delicate science, and one that is fraught with risk.

Given that movements are fueled by human passion, they're not something to be trifled with or taken lightly. Generally speaking, members of a movement are hungry for meaning and authenticity, which tends to put movements at odds with superficiality and commercialism. Moreover, marketers should know that movements are about "insiders" and "outsiders," and if you're an outsider trying to cozy up to a movement, you may be seen as the worst kind of outsider: a possible infiltrator.

But that doesn't mean you have to remain on the sidelines, watching the movement march past you. It is possible for an outsider to become an insider, to become a trusted and valued member of the community—if you're willing to earn that trust and prove that value. In the chapters ahead, we'll look at some of the critical steps (such as the five basic ones shown in Figure 1-3) that are required to build a movement from the ground up.

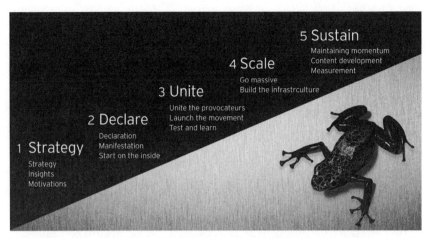

Figure 1-3 **The Five Phases of Movement Marketing**

We'll look inside a number of today's most dynamic and successful cultural movements—some of them in the business world, some in the social realm, and some in between—to see why people start movements, what gives those initiatives momentum and keeps them going, and, most important, what it is that movements want and need from you. A connection to a movement can be the best thing that ever happened to your company or your brand (even if you're a brand of one). And in the best of circumstances, you can do much more than be part of a movement—you can actually become a movement yourself.

WHY PEOPLE HAVE ALWAYS BEEN DRAWN TO MOVEMENTS

While the movement phenomenon is growing, it's certainly not new. The instinct to band together in groups is hardwired in all of us. From earliest times, humans' propensity to gather and work together to achieve a common purpose or goal was critical to our survival and our advancement as a species. And it's no less critical in today's world, where we depend on peers, collaborators, and fellow members of our "tribe" to help us keep up with constant change, increased complexity, and seemingly endless choices and challenges.

But until fairly recently, forming large groups was not an easy thing to do, and turning a group into something that could actually be called a movement was harder still. To be organized enough to be able to take collective action required group members to be able to overcome barriers of separation and the complexities of trying to communicate and organize. People had to find places and opportunities to come together and efficient ways to disseminate information.

New technology has lowered, if not removed, most of those old barriers. Now, like-minded souls can find one another with a few keystrokes. Through social networking, groups can organize overnight, and can share information immediately and constantly.

Of course, the new tools are only part of the story. The rest, it seems, is about a growing hunger for meaning, for a sense of belonging and purpose in a complex and challenging world. The newfound ability to network and take collective action has fueled a growing desire among people to express themselves in new ways, to take a stand on issues, and to tackle social problems. More and more people have begun to engage with and shape the culture around them, as opposed to being passive "consumers" of a culture created for them by others.

MOVEMENT ADVOCACY PARTNERSHIP

EXEMPLAR ONE CAMPAIGN

THE BIG IDEA ONE is a broad-based antipoverty movement designed to achieve social change by high-profile collaborative advocacy. A diverse group of celebrities, nonprofit organizations, and millions of active members has banded together to issue relentless calls to action and to hold political leaders accountable to commitments they've made to change policies and improve poverty programs in Africa. The movement relies heavily on online petitions and online donations.

STARTED Bono, Bob Geldof, Bobby Shriver, Jamie Drummond, and Lucy Matthew joined forces in 2002 to start up DATA, which morphed into ONE. Ten other organizations quickly joined: Bread for the World, CARE, International Medical Corps, International Rescue Committee, Mercy Corps, Oxfam America, Plan USA, Save the Children U.S., World Concern, and World Vision.

HOW IT SPREAD Information about ONE has been spread by celebrity spokespeople (U2 front man Bono often speaks about the movement during concerts and in the media), 11 nonprofit partners, a large Internet presence, and field organizers around the United States.

WHERE IT STANDS NOW ONE has more than 2.5 million members around the world.

QUOTE "While ONE's membership presses from the outside, ONE's policy and government relations shops work on the inside, sharing ideas and on-the-ground intelligence from Africa and across the G8 with policymakers and providing their staffs with the in-depth research necessary to buttress our arguments."

WEBSITE One.org/us/

The author Clay Shirky has observed that this confluence of new communications technology with a growing desire to engage and make a statement is resulting in "the most radical spread of expressive capability in human history." Much of that human expression is happening in groups engaged in what Shirky calls "shared endeavors." Or to think of it another way, what we're seeing is an explosion of movements, some large and some very small.

These mini-movements—bringing together crafties, locavores, or Christian rockers—may not have the magnitude or scope of what we normally think of as social movements, such as the civil rights movement. Nor are they necessarily giving birth to revolutionary new forms of expression (the Etsy craft movement is a far cry from the Renaissance).

But they are, nevertheless, highly passionate undertakings for those involved in them. And they can and often do bring about cultural change in some form. That "change" element is critical, in my view. If a public groundswell occurs without altering people's attitudes or shifting the cultural dialogue at least slightly, then it's not a movement—it's just a fad.

THE PSYCHOLOGY BEHIND MOVEMENTS

To understand cultural movements, you must understand the people within them—the folks who start movements, who join them, and who push them toward the goal of changing the world around us. What do they have in common, across all of these diverse passions and causes? What makes them want to join a movement, commit to a shared endeavor, and spread the word to others? In the coming chapters, you will meet larger-than-life characters who are altering the way we live, eat, age, teach, protect animals, take care of the planet, improve communities, solve problems, and conduct business. There is a lot to learn about, and from, these people and the ways they think, interact, and generate forward progress. Forget the stereotypes of wild-eyed activists. What you'll see, I hope, is that the people who join and propel movements have the same passions, hopes, and dreams as the rest of us. The difference is that they act, they engage, and they rise to the challenge.

The sociologist Neil Smelser has theorized that social movements come about because of a combination of factors, starting with social strain. In the most extreme cases, this strain may take the form of oppression, which, in turn, can spark revolutionary uprisings. But today's mini-movements are more often a response to a sense of dissatisfaction, restlessness, and concern about the future. In later chapters we'll explore the reasons why people join movements, what they hope to get out of it, and what the movement, if it is to grow and be successful, must offer these "true believers."

One of the key things to keep in mind is that most movements, particularly the kind that are springing up more and more in today's digitally connected environment, are very democratic. They may or may not have a clear leader—case in point, the famously "leaderless" Occupy Wall Street movement. But even if they do, much of what happens within the group is determined by the complex and fascinating interactions among members. The way the members of a movement pass along information, share tasks, and look to one another for cues often mimics what happens in nature's swarms of insects or birds (indeed, the striking parallels between swarm theory and movement dynamics are explored in Chapter 4). The most important point to bear in mind is that nothing influences members of a group as much as other members do.

MOVEMENT BICYCLE ADVOCACY

EXEMPLAR CRITICAL MASS

THE BIG IDEA Critical Mass celebrates bicycling and bikers' rights to have access to the public streets. A Critical Mass ride is created when a group of riders comes together for a few hours every month to take back the streets of a city.

STARTED Critical Mass was started in San Francisco in 1992.

HOW IT SPREAD The rides are publicized by local flyers, banners, and T-shirts; in community pages on the Critical Mass wiki or local websites; and on list serves in individual cities.

WHERE IT STANDS NOW It is estimated that Critical Mass rides have taken place in close to 350 cities around the world. Many other bicycling movements have come out of the Critical Mass rides. Meanwhile, pushback from cities seems to have curtailed the movement in some places.

QUOTE "Some people see Critical Mass as a forum for grassroots political change. Some people see it as a protest against cars. Some people just like to ride."—Critical Mass

WEBSITE Wikipedia.org/wiki/Critical_Mass

Meanwhile, the amount of influence that flows out of the group—to the world that exists outside the movement—can be huge. Movement members tend to be digitally connected, socially engaged, and vocal. And while it's generally understood that today, anyone who is actively using social media has "three degrees of influence" (extending from the individual to all connected "friends," and ultimately to the friends of those friends), members of movements are more apt to have socially engaged friends who belong to other movements, which means that the circles of influence that emanate from a movement are likely to include many related and overlapping movements.

In addition, the passion and energy of movements tends to draw attention from those outside the circle, including the press. As a result, a movement can spread the word about something more efficiently and with greater credibility than any form of advertising.

This brings us back to why understanding and connecting with movements is so critical to the success of marketing and, by extension, the future of business. Movement marketing represents a potentially game-changing way for brands to connect with people's lives and passions. And yet, almost everything about the nature of movements, and the people who join them, suggests that this phenomenon might not bode well for marketers. For instance, people who are actively and passionately engaged in community endeavors are harder to reach than an audience that sits passively in front of a TV, absorbing commercial messages. And people whose views and behaviors are most likely to be influenced by their peers—by fellow members of the "swarm"—are less likely to be influenced by messages from an outside entity that has no connection to the causes, issues, and passions of the movement.

TURNING CONVENTIONAL MARKETING APPROACHES UPSIDE-DOWN

Therefore, what's required is nothing less than a radical rethinking on the part of marketers and business leaders. Movement marketing takes the old marketing and business models and flips them on their heads. For example:

- Instead of marketing and advertising being focused on "the individual," as they have been for decades, we're entering new territory in which marketers must learn to understand and relate to people in interconnected groups.

- Instead of attempting to persuade people to believe an ad message, marketers must try to tap into what it is that people *already* believe and care about.

- Instead of being focused on *selling*, the way to connect with movements is to be dedicated to *sharing*.

- Instead of controlling the message, marketers must learn to relinquish control and let the movement do what it will with that message.

- Perhaps most radical of all, companies and brands must learn to stop talking about themselves and to join in a conversation that is about anything and everything *but* their product.

All of this may seem counterintuitive from a business standpoint. It introduces elements of risk and unpredictability into the marketing process. It goes against B-school rules and the top-down traditions of corporate culture.

But if a company can navigate this new landscape; if it can ditch the sales pitch, recognizing that it is now more important to influence the group than to persuade the individual; and if it can learn to be as passionate about big ideas and important causes as its potential customers are—if it can do all of these things, that company can quickly find itself riding a powerful wave that will carry it into the future. I know all this is possible because over the past decade, StrawberryFrog has helped companies and brands of all sizes and shapes to successfully ride the wave of cultural movements. We began using this cultural movement approach with entrepreneurial brands based in Europe back in 1999. But as you'll see in the case studies throughout the book, we've been able to employ it with larger, established brands around the world. Most recently, this approach and the whole concept of movements have been drawing the interest of some of the biggest global names in business, such as Procter & Gamble, PepsiCo, Emirates Airlines, Natura of Brasil, and Mahindra of India—all of which have begun working with us on the process of shifting their marketing strategy to focus more on the power of movements.

If the giants of the business world—companies that have a great deal invested in the traditional marketing model—can begin to make this transformation, then smaller and leaner companies can also do it, probably with a lot less effort. In the end, I believe, companies large and small will have to come to terms with this dramatic shift in the culture and in the lives of their customers.

THE BASIC DOS AND DON'TS

In the chapters ahead, we'll work through some of the fundamental dos and don'ts of movement marketing. A few of the key points to be covered include:

- **"SHARING IS THE NEW CURRENCY."** As the futurist Johansen has observed, sharing is becoming paramount in business. Companies (or entrepreneurs, politicians, or community leaders) can connect with movements by helping to *facilitate* those movements. Only by doing this can you be seen as an ally of the movement, rather than a usurper. The secret to doing this is to figure out how to create what Johansen calls "commons," which can take the form of shared media platforms, facilities, resources, expert information, content, software, or ideas—anything that can be of use in helping people to connect with one another and advance the goals of a particular movement. In the book, we'll explore how businesses are in a position to share all kinds of commons—there are dozens, perhaps hundreds of possible ways to help facilitate movements, using resources that a company may not even know it has.

- **THE IMPORTANCE OF "QUIET TRANSPARENCY."** To earn credibility within movements and communities, companies must do the right thing, be transparent about it, and eschew self-promotion and hype. If you advertise yourself, you're elevating your agenda over that of the movement.

- **THE KEYS TO IDENTIFYING "IDEAS ON THE RISE" IN CULTURE.** To get a better sense of what's going on out there in the world of those people you're trying to connect with, you have to pay attention to what they're talking about, what's affecting their lives, and what's fueling their dreams and passions.

- **FIGURING OUT WHERE YOUR BRAND OR COMPANY FITS INTO THE CONVERSATION.** What is the intersection between your brand and a cause or issue that people care about? (Hint: Before you take a stand, you'll want to clarify what it is your company actually stands for.)

- **IN-GROUPS, OUT-GROUPS, AND IDENTIFYING THE "BAD GUY."**
  Companies pursuing movement marketing must figure out
  whom they care most about and which potential customer
  groups they may be willing to sacrifice, while also deciding
  who or what they're prepared to attack as a "cultural nemesis."

- **UNDERSTANDING WHO'S IN CHARGE.** In movement marketing, companies must be prepared to give up a certain amount
  of control of their message, which is never easy. But there are
  important things a brand can do to ensure that the message
  stays positive and that the uprising doesn't end up being against
  you. Business can take a lesson from politics here: as we'll see
  in Chapter 7, the groundbreaking Dean primary campaign, and
  later the Obama campaign, shows us how a willingness to turn
  over control can create a bottom-up, self-organizing system
  that is autonomous, passionate, and self-sustaining.

- **HOW TO LIGHT THE SPARK.** People assume that movements
  just happen. But we'll examine how the conditions that ignite
  an uprising can be identified and, in some cases, encouraged.
  The "commons" you share, the platform you provide, or any
  number of contributing factors you add to the mix can serve as
  the X factor that brings a movement to life or enables it to grow.

While the idea of "movement marketing" may be new, the
phenomenon of people rallying around brands is not. In the next
chapter, we'll take a look at how a number of brands over the past
half century have been able to spark movements that have had a
profound impact on the culture—to say nothing of the transforma-
tional effects they had on those companies.

CHAPTER 2

From "Thinking Small" to Getting "Real"

A BRIEF HISTORY OF MOVEMENTS AND BRANDS

It's 1960, and you're flipping through *Life* magazine. You're stopped by an advertisement that doesn't look like any of the other ads in the magazine. There's lots of white space, a tiny off-center image of the car itself (which, by the way, is an odd-looking little vehicle), and an understated two-word headline, "Think small."

The ad stands out because this isn't what ads are supposed to be like in 1960. It's neither splashy nor dreamy; it has none of those familiar ad images of folks laughing and frolicking, women's hair blowing in the breeze, gorgeous scenery—all those too-good-to-be-true images that were associated with ads at the time. Moreover, the ad seems to be speaking a new language: it's more straightforward and down-to-earth than ad copy is supposed to be, but at the same time, it's also smarter, sharper, and more clever.

Just from reading the ad, you feel like maybe you get some sense of the people who made it, as well as the people who made the car. They're not like everybody else; they seem to be zigging while all others are zagging—which is kind of the way you see yourself. In a time of conformity and "keeping up with the Joneses," this ad is about going your own way. You may or not buy this car, but there's something going on in this ad that you're connecting with, and that you might want to be part of.

The Volkswagen "Think Small" campaign is widely recognized as the ad that helped launch advertising's creative revolution of the 1960s. But I think it was something else, too. It may well have been the first time a marketer successfully launched a movement behind a brand.

Mind you, it was clearly different from some of the more modern marketing movements we'll be looking at throughout this book—for one thing, it was much simpler in terms of how it communicated with the public. Obviously, VW's ad agency, Doyle Dane Bernbach (DDB) couldn't use Facebook or Twitter or any of the other marvelous social networking tools that are now so integral to launching movements; it relied on a series of striking print ads, some very memorable TV commercials, and a billboard here and there.

But even if VW and DDB weren't wired and digitally networked at the time, they did, nonetheless, have a good ear to the ground. And that enabled them to pick up the early rumblings of something that was just starting to build at that time—a vague dissatisfaction with 1950s consumerism and the prevailing "bigger is better" mindset about cars. The 1960s counterculture had not yet taken hold, but there was a restlessness out there—which no one in the mainstream culture had really expressed prior to this—about big fins and gas-guzzling Cadillacs, and what all of that represented.

Dominik Imseng, the author of *Think Small*, a book about the famous ad, notes that there was something "un-American" about it (and not just because the car was made in Germany). "In a way," Imseng says, "'Think Small' was Ginsberg's *Howl* from 1956 as an ad—objecting to the consumerism and materialism of the American Way of Life."

Julian Koenig, one of the ad's original creators, said that part of the idea he was trying to convey was that in buying a Volkswagen, "You could take an inverse delight in not having to keep up with the Joneses—in not responding to Detroit's planned obsolescence, in not being part of that repetitive, competitive culture."

Certainly, America was ready for an alternative in terms of car choices, and the Volkswagen Beetle offered that alternative. But a product by itself does not a movement make. People tend to gather and rally around ideas, and usually those ideas have to be expressed in a certain way to get folks fired up. This is the reason why social movements are often associated with iconic images, symbols, or flags; it's also the reason why many movements develop rallying cries, phrases and words that come to mean something very deep to the people within the movement.

The Volkswagen campaign was rich in the kind of semiotics that can serve as shorthand for communicating a radical idea to large numbers of people who are receptive to it. DDB designer

Helmut Krone's use of white space in the "Think Small" ad was almost an act of defiance, in advertising terms. Why would an advertiser pay for that space and then leave it empty? Krone was sending a signal to his audience: "We don't care about ad conventions, and neither do you, so let's dispense with unnecessary imagery." Similar nod-and-wink messages could be picked up from the way the car was depicted in the ads (shrunken down and off-center; in one ad, Krone even showed the car dented!). Along with the understated style of the copy, it all said to the ad's audience, "There's something going on here, not just in this ad, but in the culture. Do you get it? Are you part of it?"

Those who could tune in to those messages, who understood the cultural changes that VW was talking about and agreed with the basic philosophy behind "Think Small," became the "true believers" of the movement. VW had created a kind of club to which these people could belong. And those who became part of that club weren't just customers—they were advocates who took up the cause. They came to embrace VW's ideals, identified with the brand, and, in many cases, remained loyal to it for years and even decades to come.

WHY THE THINKING BEHIND "THINK SMALL" IS STILL RELEVANT

Today, a half century later, there's a lot we can learn from "Think Small"—and also from subsequent groundbreaking campaigns from Apple Computer, Diesel Jeans, and Dove soap—about how to connect with people in a way that goes beyond just selling a product. One key point is that for any marketing campaign to go beyond being just ads and generate something that can credibly be called a movement, there must be a powerful idea at the core—one that is about a lot more than just the product you're trying to sell.

MOVEMENT CAUSE MARKETING

EXEMPLAR   (PRODUCT) RED CAMPAIGN

THE BIG IDEA Cause marketing is a partnership between for-profits and nonprofits for mutual benefit. It offers causes valuable branding and visibility for all concerned. (PRODUCT) RED's goal is to transform the collective power of consumers into a financial force to help fight AIDS and other diseases in Africa. (RED) is a brand licensed to partner with companies such as the Gap, Nike, Starbucks, Converse, Dell, Apple, American Express, and Penguin Classics, among others. These companies develop their own product(s) featuring the high-profile (PRODUCT) RED logo, with a percentage of the proceeds going to the Global Fund to Fight AIDS, tuberculosis, and malaria.

STARTED Bono of U2 and Bobby Shriver founded (PRODUCT) RED in 2006.

HOW IT SPREAD (PRODUCT) RED spread through its pacts with its partners, extensive media coverage resulting from the high profile of the corporations involved and (PRODUCT) RED's founders, social networking, celebrity spokespeople, and brand exposure. In 2010, a full-length documentary called *The Lazarus Effect* was executive produced by Spike Jonze and sponsored by (RED), HBO, and Anonymous Content, on the heels of a public-service TV campaign (of the same name) featuring high-profile celebrities in the United States.

WHERE IT STANDS NOW (RED) has generated more than $170 million and has reached more than 7.5 million people in Ghana, Lesotho, Rwanda, South Africa, Swaziland, and Zambia. Programs supported by the Global Fund have averted 6.5 million deaths worldwide.

QUOTE "The shoppers who've chosen (RED) and the companies who've turned (RED) are heroes. Each individual's decision is saving the lives of more than 30,000 AIDS patients in Rwanda and Swaziland today and ensuring that HIV-positive pregnant mothers receive the medicine they need." —Bobby Shriver, cofounder

WEBSITE JoinRed.com/red

Marketers aren't used to thinking this way—they certainly weren't back then and, for the most part, they still aren't today. The conventional way a marketer approaches his or her challenge is to think, "I've got a product to sell, and I need to convince people that it is better than any other competing product out there." This usually leads to boastful (and not particularly credible or compelling) claims about the superiority of features that people may not care much about anyway. To try to raise the interest level a bit, marketers are likely to throw in suggestive imagery: "Buy this car, and you can live out your fantasies." The creative minds behind VW were smart enough to know that they couldn't sell a humble little car by using a lot of product hype and fantasy. That led them to more of a grounded, real-world approach to marketing the car. But it also forced them to grapple with issues such as, "All the advertising BS aside, what does this car stand for?" and "How does that connect with what's happening in the culture right now?"

Maybe the most radical thing that "Think Small" did was take a stand *against* something—actually, against most of what was accepted and popular in American culture at the time. Again, this defies the conventional marketing mindset, which generally aims to please everyone and offend no one. But the reality is, it may be impossible to generate a passionate movement that appeals to everyone—by their very nature, movements tend to be *for* something and *against* something else.

A good movement, if it's successful, does something else, too: it brings about change. Not necessarily huge change, like a government overthrow (although, of course, sometimes a movement does that as well). But even a humble marketing movement, if it's worth the name, ought to alter perceptions and shift the cultural dialogue at least a little. Obviously, the Volkswagen campaign shifted the way we thought about a number of things: cars, status symbols, consumerism, and, of course, advertising. After "Think Small," many people looked at ads a little differently, including the people who made ads—who were inspired to start their own movement within the ad industry to bring more creativity to the business overall.

THE NEXT MAJOR UPRISING—THIS TIME, AGAINST BIG BROTHER

But even though the Volkswagen campaign helped trigger an uprising that yielded many wonderfully creative ads in the 1960s and early 1970s, none of them quite matched "Think Small" as a stellar example of early movement marketing. It was about two decades before another marketer not only reached that level, but went even further in terms of staking out a position and inspiring consumers to join in and be part of a revolution. I'm talking, of course, about the movement that was sparked and led by Apple Computer.

When we think of Apple, we think of great, groundbreaking products—and with good reason. With its introductions of the Apple II and subsequently the Macintosh, Apple "enabled people to do things they couldn't do before, and that can be a big reason why people join a movement," says Guy Kawasaki, the former "chief evangelist" at Apple and a key figure in its early rise.

But as Kawasaki and others acknowledge, there was also something more than great products at work. John Scully, the company's former president, observed to the press, "People talk about technology, but Apple was a marketing company. It was the marketing company of the decade." And its marketing approach involved building a movement, starting with the true believers and early fanatics who would become Apple's advocates and evangelists.

When I spoke to Kawasaki, he maintained that much of the early creation of the cult of Apple happened by circumstances more than by design. "The movement happened almost *despite* Apple in some sense," Kawasaki says. He notes that Apple back then—and even today—never believed much in "the social aspects of building a movement." Steve Jobs was always intensely private, and the company has never gone out of its way to make outsiders—fans, journalists, or bloggers—feel that they were part of what the company was doing. But nevertheless, hundreds and eventually thousands of user groups self-formed and, according to Kawasaki, became the "true evangelists" who tried to convince other like-minded people to climb aboard the Apple bandwagon.

In Jobs, Apple had the kind of charismatic leader that can draw people to a movement. Moreover, the company and its products seemed to represent something that a certain kind of person wanted to be a part of. It broke the mold of how companies were run at the time; it developed products that were unique; it was, in a word, cool. The psychologist Ross Goldstein studied Apple customers at one point, and, as he told *Wired* magazine, the attachment was deep and at least as emotional as it was logical. Among these true believers, "there was a profound sense that Apple was one of them—counterculture, grassroots, human, approachable. Apple really appeals to the humanistic side of people."

It didn't hurt that the company cast itself in the role of underdog to IBM, which seemed to represent big-business corporate values. "People are drawn to the underdog, but it also depends on *underdog to whom?*" says Kawasaki. "If you're an underdog to Nordstrom or Virgin America, that's different from being underdog to IBM and Microsoft, who seem as if they're trying to control the world. So yes, we had a good foil."

As for the semiotics used to transmit the message, a lot of that could be found in the actual design of the products, particularly the playful and accessible user interface. But when Apple introduced the Macintosh with the famous Chiat/Day commercial "1984," there was no shortage of symbolism and iconic imagery, all playing off the idea that IBM represented Big Brother, while Apple was leading a technology revolution that was going to set people free. By this time, the true believers were already on board; "1984" was aimed at the rest of us, to let us know there was something going on out there.

A FANATICISM THAT BORDERS
ON THE RELIGIOUS

So how strong was the bond that Apple formed with the members of its growing movement? For one thing, it was strong enough to keep people faithful even as the company struggled through various product misfires and failures (yes, Apple did have its share of failures through the years, although people may not remember that now). It was strong enough to keep people engaged and interested even when the charismatic leader Jobs left for a spell, to wander in the desert. In a way, the whole Jobs saga, complete with crucifixion and resurrection, only served to strengthen the movement by providing it with a dramatic story and mythology.

Today, the true believers are as faithful as ever—the only thing that has changed is the size of their ranks. Time and again, we see the same scenes the world over when Apple launches a product. People travel for miles and camp overnight outside stores to get their hands on the latest offering—no matter what the cost. Note that Apple never uses special offers or discounts to create this type of impact; it's purely product power and the special feeling of being the first to have the latest from Apple's core that drives it. A recent documentary film explored Apple's power and found that its fans' reactions to its products bordered on the religious. In the film, researchers conducted an experiment: in one corner, an Apple fan; in another, a religious believer. The results of an MRI scan showed that Apple was actually stimulating the same parts of the brain as religious imagery does in people of faith.

One could surmise that the reason that Apple and Volkswagen were able to build movements was that they were offering exceptional, truly distinctive, and groundbreaking products. But a popular product, in and of itself, does not necessarily create a movement; if anything, it's more likely to trigger a fad (see the sidebar "Pokémon Versus Wii").

There's no doubt that the Beetle and the Macintosh were the kinds of product offerings that stand out—and that people can fall in love with. But what about something as generic as a pair of jeans? Or as basic as a bar of soap? Is it possible to get people to rally around and feel passionate about products that aren't necessarily revolutionary?

FROM DIESEL . . .

I was in the early years of my advertising career and happened to be working in Sweden when, during the early 1990s, a Swedish agency (where I didn't work) was cooking up a global campaign for an Italian fashion brand called Diesel. Known primarily for making jeans and other hip, youth-oriented apparel, Diesel took the marketing world by storm when that agency, Paradiset DDB, launched a series of ads that seemed to make no sense to some people. The ads promoted themselves as offering "a guide to successful living for people interested in general health and mental power." And in each individual ad, the suggested way to improve the world was as absurd and ironic as that general theme. One purported to offer a solution to the problem of "how to control wild animals" by proposing that we "build more zoos"—so that we can then use the available wilderness for shopping malls and golf courses. Other ads featured politicians in diapers, sinister-looking dentists, and sun-worshipping senior citizens offering ironic tips on how to get rich or get a suntan. Some ventured into controversial territory, such as gun use.

While the ads were simply baffling to some, others got the message: Diesel was making fun of advertising itself. The brand was tapping into a restless dissatisfaction, particularly among young people, with the imagery and messages that were being foisted on them constantly—everything from vapid fashion models to what I would call the "Wrigley spearmint gum" school of ads, chock-full of fresh-faced types laughing and running around on beaches. Diesel's marketers sensed that young people had had their fill of this hype, even if they had no way of articulating that dissatisfaction. So Diesel created a different kind of hype that was, essentially, an inside joke on advertising. The campaign's co-creator, Joakim Jonason, said the ads were intended as a satire on an ad business that is, "at its worst, full of empty promises."

Ads that poke fun of advertising are fairly common now, but at the time they weren't. And because Diesel never actually *said* that it was mocking advertising—the ads were purposely vague—the semiotics of the campaign took the form of over-the-top imagery and ironic language. Either you picked up the signals Diesel was sending or you shook your head and muttered, "What's this all about?" If you were in the former group, you became part of the Diesel movement that propelled this obscure fashion brand to instant success. And the more other people (including clueless parents) complained about those crazy ads, the more the "insiders" felt that they were in the know and special.

... TO DOVE

Even more successful (and a lot more coherent) than the Diesel campaign was the mid-2000s "Real Beauty" campaign for Dove soap. By featuring women of all body types, who didn't look like typical advertising models, Dove took on advertising stereotypes just as Diesel had done—but it did so in a manner that was celebratory and inspirational, rather than ironic.

Like Diesel, Dove sensed that there was a growing dissatisfaction out there, this time among women regarding the portrayals of the female body in ads. To explore this more deeply, the company did extensive research up front, commissioning a study called "The Real Truth about Beauty" to try to get a better sense of what women were feeling. What became clear was that many wanted to see images in the media that were more realistic and more representative of all body types. Still, it was a bold decision for Dove to act on this by creating ads that featured nonmodels of all shapes and sizes, provocatively posed and shot as if they were supermodels.

Kevin George, who was part of the brand team at Unilever that worked on the campaign, says: "It was born out of a common insight that no one ever wanted to talk about, which was that most women didn't look like the models in the magazine—they looked like real people, and they were beautiful in a natural way." The Dove marketers also realized that the concept was actually one that made sense for Dove soap. This is a concept that we'll explore more throughout the book: that for an "idea on the rise" to be most effective as a brand movement, the idea should somehow intersect with the attributes and values of the brand. In the case of Dove, "the products we made were designed to bring out the real beauty in women, not try to change them to be what they thought they should be," George says. "That small insight went to a place that was totally different for a beauty brand: to say, 'You're beautiful as you are. We're not going to try to change you, just to bring out the beauty you already have.' And that spoke to so many women, who then wanted to be a part of this idea."

The campaign did what a good movement should do: it spurred cultural dialogue, and began to shift attitudes and perceptions. The *Adweek* columnist Barbara Lippert commented at the time that the campaign "goes against what everybody did for 50 years, which is make you anxious about how you look. . . . This is saying, 'You're good enough.'" It had an impact within the ad business, too, as imitators quickly surfaced with their own versions of "real women" campaigns. Oh, and by the way, it worked incredibly well from a sales standpoint, too, increasing the sales of products featured in the ads by 600 percent in the first two months. During its first year, more than a million people went to the "campaignforrealbeauty" website to find out more and share their thoughts about the campaign.

After the strong initial reaction to the ads, Dove expanded "Real Beauty" into a full-fledged movement that gave its followers and admirers lots of ways to engage, participate, and be inspired. In 2006, the company created the Dove Self-Esteem Fund, with the stated goal of trying to broaden the Western concept of female beauty while encouraging girls and women of all body types to take pride in their appearance. The ads were supplemented by online films focused on the self-esteem theme, including the award-winning film *Evolution*.

Looking at the Volkswagen, Apple, Diesel, and Dove movements together, what can be said about all of them? They picked up on themes that people had strong, largely unarticulated feelings about at the time. They expressed these ideas and attitudes in a way that resonated with people. They gave those who agreed with the idea something to rally around or get behind. And they helped bring about change on some level, if only by altering perceptions or ways of thinking about a given subject. Maybe most important (from the marketers' standpoint, at least), they formed a bond that was stronger than the usual connection between brand and customer because it was based on more than the buying and selling of products. It was rooted in a sense of shared values, as in, "This brand stands for something; what's more, it has taken a stand for something, and now I've taken that stand with it."

MOVEMENT CAUSE MARKETING

EXEMPLAR GO FORTH

THE BIG IDEA Go Forth is an international movement, started by the Levi's brand, to champion and support "creative, courageous, selfless individuals who are helping to make the world a better place." These individuals are called "pioneers" and are profiled in Levi's ad campaigns as well as on the Go Forth website. The hope is to inspire others to emulate them, while associating the brand with youth, optimism, and activism.

STARTED Go Forth was started by Wieden+Kennedy for Levi's in 2009.

HOW IT SPREAD As with any ad campaign, its greatest exposure is via TV and print. The Levi's Legacy YouTube channel has tens of thousands of subscribers who see the ads, which are shot by top directors, as soon as they are uploaded. On the Go Forth website, pioneers are profiled and viewers are asked to tweet their support, thus spreading the word on both the individuals' mission and the Go Forth/Levi's brand.

WHERE IT STANDS NOW   The campaign went global in August 2011 with a print, film, and social media campaign that used words from writer Charles Bukowski's uplifting poem "The Laughing Heart" to frame a series of shots of hopeful youth in Berlin in an effort to inspire positive engagement with the future. Levi's also sponsored a series of murals in Berlin by Portuguese street artist Vhils. Go Forth is highlighted on the Levi's corporate website and Facebook page (more than 7 million followers), with a strong call to *get involved*.

QUOTE   "Go Forth is about embodying the energy and events of our time, it is not about any specific movement or political theme; rather, it's about optimism, positive action and a pioneering spirit." —Levi's

WEBSITE   Goforth.levi.com/en

I think it's easy to see why this kind of bond is important and why it can create loyal customers and evangelists. This was true half a century ago, back at the dawn of "Think Small." But if you think the social themes addressed in the Volkswagen campaign are any less relevant today, take a look at StrawberryFrog's recent campaign for Smart Car (see the sidebar "From Anti-big to Anti-dumb"), which puts a more modern eco-conscious twist on the idea of thinking small, and which has generated a very powerful movement on behalf of Smart.

THE POSTPRODUCT ERA

Not only is this approach to marketing still relevant, but I believe that today it's more important than ever for brands to try to connect with people in this way—on a level that transcends just trying to sell them products. And the reason it matters more now is that we're in a postproduct era of marketing. The old model of selling products based on a "unique selling proposition" has gradually become outdated because, with more and more product parity, there usually isn't anything that's all that unique about most products—and those that do manage to find a new innovation are likely to see it quickly imitated and adopted by others. With distinctions and improvements in product benefits being so incremental now, your brand has to stand for something more than just the product. That new button or feature doesn't matter all that much unless the brand itself matters to people. And I would argue that before your brand can really matter to people, you first need to understand all the other things that really matter to them.

My own first encounter with the power of movements came in Europe, where I established StrawberryFrog, far removed from the marketing conventions of Madison Avenue. I had the task of helping clients such as the groundbreaking furniture retailer IKEA (whose brand movement was energized by the founder's passsion that not only the rich deserve beautiful furniture) to break through in markets where television advertising budgets were limited. We were forced to experiment with various "guerrilla marketing" tactics, trying to figure out how to get unexpected, compelling messages to people in unconventional ways. Out of necessity, we embraced the Internet in its early days—while Madison Avenue was still doing its best to ignore this new medium.

What I learned early on was that the web wasn't a particularly effective tool when it came to broadcasting ad messages. To try to use this connective, interactive medium as just another form of TV was a mistake that many marketers at the time fell prey to (and, incredibly, many of them are still making this mistake today!). But the web was ideally suited for a different kind of marketing—one that focused on community building, two-way conversations, and figuring out what people were truly interested in and cared about.

And what people really cared about, I found, usually had little to do with products and more to do with ideas—with interesting trends, new ways of thinking about and looking at the world, or fresh ways of expressing oneself. Young people in particular were hungry for these new ideas and influences; they gravitated toward them, immersed themselves in them, and shared them with friends. As they did this, they were often joining, or sometimes creating, small cultural movements.

CONNECTING WITH "IDEAS ON THE RISE"

We felt that if we could somehow associate a brand with a larger idea that was just beginning to gain traction in the culture (by associating, say, a nearly forgotten Japanese running shoe with the sudden resurgence of Japanese retro culture), we could enable the brand to rise up alongside that idea. Once you've identified that big cultural idea, you must figure out how to bring it to life, give it a unique expression, and allow people to engage with it and be part of it—and all of that must be done subtly and respectfully. There's a fine line between associating with a rising idea and trying to co-opt it or turn it into a banal sales pitch. We had to support and foster these burgeoning movements quietly, rather than be seen as exploiting or hijacking them (a surefire way to kill a rising idea or movement). We gradually constructed a communications model tailored to the particular requirements of movement marketing.

MOVEMENT CAUSE MARKETING

EXEMPLAR LET'S COLOUR PROJECT

THE BIG IDEA Paint company Dulux transforms communities by sending volunteers to gray corners of the world and enlivening them with a fresh coat of paint. They collaborate with local communities to find and paint schools, streets, homes, and squares. The project is not just about filming a commercial, but leaving something behind that actually changes places and people's outlooks.

STARTED Euro RSCG started Let's Colour for Dulux in March 2010.

HOW IT SPREAD Let's Colour started with projects in four countries—Brazil, France, the United Kingdom, and India—and garnered local publicity wherever it went. The Let's Colour blog documents all the locales, with filmmaker Adam Berg and his crew filming the transformations. The videos of the events became commercials, and ultimately were turned into a documentary about the local people that participated in the projects. Let's Colour posted more than 50 short videos on YouTube, relying on social sharing to spread the word. The Let's Colour blog features several of these inspirational videos about the early days of the movement, including a cool two-minute time-lapse video/ad that captures the locales getting trans-formed by color almost by magic.

WHERE IT STANDS NOW   Since the initial four projects, the Let's Colour Project has visited four more worldwide locations (there have been no new projects since 2010). The website has the usual Get Involved and Tell Your Friends pages to encourage social sharing.

QUOTE   "The Let's Colour Project is based on an invitation, the invitation to colour. Thus, it can't and it shouldn't only happen when we promote events; it must take a life of its own, it is a movement, and a movement only happens if loads of people join in. Through social media, we can make sure more and more people learn about how fantastic it is to live with colour, how it lifts one's mood, how it brings gray spaces some happiness." —Fernanda Romano, Euro RSCG Worldwide

WEBSITE   Letscolourproject.com

Along the way, we made some of the mistakes that market-ers are prone to make in this new landscape. I discuss these at length in the chapters ahead, because these missteps provide good and useful lessons. Meanwhile, our success stories began to add up. SmartCar, Heineken, Mitsubishi, Pfizer, Coca-Cola, Walmart, Google, Microsoft—we found that no matter what a company might be offering, there was a way to find or spark a movement that made sense for that product and/or brand.

Gradually, as the little European agency known as StrawberryFrog continued to grow beyond Europe into South America, we also put down roots in New York and brought the "movement movement" to the heart of Madison Avenue. We saw ourselves as a small and agile frog amid the dinosaurs of advertising.

THE MOVEMENT COMES TO MAD. AVE.

We quickly discovered that the big traditional Madison Avenue marketing companies hadn't changed much over the years— although the world all around them sure had. By the mid- to late 2000s, it was clear that the old marketing model, based on slogans and overpriced 30-second TV spots, had grown creaky and ineffi- cient. Meanwhile, the technological and sociological changes that had first made movement marketing viable a few years earlier had by now shifted into a much higher gear. Facebook, YouTube, Twitter, Foursquare—if I myself had been designing tools that could possibly take movement marketing to another level, I couldn't have done better than these.

The social networking revolution of the past few years has also done more than I ever could in terms of convincing the business world that it is finally time to completely reinvent the ways in which businesses communicate with the public. That may explain why some of the biggest companies in business, such as Procter & Gamble and PepsiCo, have now begun to work with us on the process of shifting their marketing strategy to focus on the power of movements.

This is a big shift for those marketers, because in order to do this right, you need to reverse the marketing process. Instead of starting with a focus on the product and trying to figure out how to make it appealing to the consumer and the culture, we tend to start with the culture (see Figure 2-1).

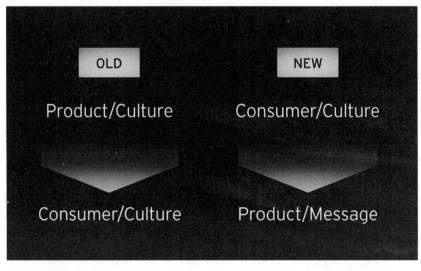

Figure 2-1

So rather than starting with this: "We've got a phone to sell; how do we get people to buy this product? What's the USP? It's got a new button here—how do we market that?" Instead, we started with this: "What's going on in the world? What's on people's minds? What is culturally relevant?"

In Chapter 5 I'll talk in greater detail about how you find and identify these "ideas on the rise," but suffice it to say that you have to do what Volkswagen and DDB did in 1960, what Apple and its marketing partners did in the early 1980s, and what Diesel did a decade later and Dove a decade after that: you have to put an ear to the ground and pick up on what people are thinking, feeling, and talking about. And it's not enough to identify just any idea that's on the rise; you must find the right idea for the brand involved, one that intersects with the essence of what the brand stands for and how it's perceived.

Volkswagen, Apple, Diesel, and Dove all found ways to do this, which is why they were among the early pioneers of movement building in the marketing world. But thanks to the technological changes—and some social changes—that have taken place in just the past few years, today's marketers are actually in a much better position to tap into the power of movements. We'll look at how to make the most of the new digital tools available to us but first, in Chapter 3, I want to focus on something much more basic, involving the fundamental building blocks of any movement. I'm talking about the people who join or start movements—the "true believers" who get things going, and those followers who join in later and help enlarge the movement. Before you can digitally connect and engage with these critical partners, you need to understand what inspires and drives them. And it all starts with the question: why do they join movements? Turn to the next chapter to find out.

POKÉMON VERSUS Wii: THE DIFFERENCE BETWEEN A FAD AND A MOVEMENT

Both Pokémon and Wii leveraged video-game technology to become hugely popular very quickly. But Pokémon was a fad, while Nintendo's Wii system was (and still is) a cultural movement. What was the difference? One phenomenon shifted people's attitudes and lifestyles, while the other did not.

Pokémon may have gotten parents to stand in line and shell out money, and it certainly kept young people enthralled for a period of time. But at bottom, it was really an entertaining cartoon brought to life in video-game format, with a host of accompanying ancillary products waiting to be purchased.

On the other hand, the Wii system—the fifth and arguably most innovative console produced by Nintendo—allowed people of all ages to play together, breaking down the age barriers that were inherent in most gaming products from competitors Xbox and PlayStation. Wii captured an idea that was on the rise—that gaming wasn't just for hard-core lone gamers anymore. It could cross generational barriers and even become a social activity. This was a radical concept that caused families to reconsider the whole concept of video games and the role they could play within the household. Rather than taking kids to the latest Pixar movie, here was a stay-at-home alternative— and one that even incorporated an element of physical activity and fitness. And it wasn't just parents and young kids that were affected. Flirting took a new form when college-age students got hold of the Wii. Social functions and parties were organized around it.

As the Wii took off in the United Kingdom, some remarkable figures emerged: two-thirds of parents with kids aged 10 to 15 reported that it was encouraging their kids to exercise more, and nearly a quarter of the respondents said that it had become part of their repertoire of social activities, such as dinner parties. The Wii caused a significant shift in cultural norms, behaviors, and attitudes.

It's interesting to consider the existing social environment, along with Nintendo's marketing tactics, at the time of the launch. The console entered the marketplace in the fall of 2006, during a time of deep discontent. Parents were concerned about rising obesity levels in kids. They were observing that their children were spending more and more time on sedentary indoor activities involving video games, the Internet, and television. And parents were pretty much cut off from those activities, because they had little understanding of or interest in those games.

Nintendo addressed this issue both through the functionality of the product (which was an accessible, uncomplicated, multiplayer system that focused on shared interests like sports) and in the marketing communication used to launch the product. The company got the semiotics just right with the "Wii" name: The two lowercase i characters, resembling two people side by side, conveyed the idea of togetherness, as did the sound of the name ("we"). Nintendo also dedicated significant marketing dollars to hosting private parties for mothers, which resulted in a massive word-of-mouth campaign that spread through neighborhoods, companies, and PTA meetings.

Nintendo was smart enough to know that if it got only kids on board, it might have another fad; but if it got their moms, it would have a movement.

FROM "ANTI-BIG" TO "ANTI-DUMB"

When StrawberryFrog was asked recently to help relaunch the diminutive Smart Car in the United States, we faced a challenge not unlike the one that Volkswagen had been dealing with decades earlier. In both cases, the preceding generation of car buyers had been conditioned to think big with its vehicles, the only difference being that the big Cadillacs of the 1950s had been replaced by the even bigger SUVs of the late 1990s and 2000s. But just as in 1960, we sensed that there was something in the air—a feeling of restlessness about overconsumption and a rising interest in being a thoughtful, responsible citizen and consumer.

We wanted to tap into that feeling in the strongest way possible, because that would increase our chances of stoking people's passions and starting a movement. While we could have talked about the features and qualities of the Smart Car—affordability, efficiency, economy, reduced environmental footprint—that probably wouldn't have moved people in quite the way we wanted.

Instead, we rallied around the insight that an increasing number of people were against outsized, excessive consumerism. As we boiled down the idea some more, what emerged was a simple yet powerful declaration of principle: buyers of the Smart Car could take a stand "against dumb."

By giving people something to rail against—in the salvos we sent out, we took aim at everything from big gas-guzzling vehicles to gigantic Venti Lattes—we quickly brought together a vocal community of advocates. In a short period of time, the brand more than quadrupled its audience and sales grew 172 percent.

Marketers may be reluctant to take a stand against something because it can feel controversial or divisive. But the truth is, some of the boldest marketers have been doing this kind of thing successfully for quite a while: Apple versus "Big Brother" conformity (as represented by IBM), Diesel and Dove taking on advertising and its manipulative ways, and, of course, at the beginning, Volkswagen taking on big cars and America's "keep-up-with-the-Joneses" consumerism. The more things change, the more they stay the same.

CHAPTER 3

Why Do People Start and Join Movements?

As we've seen in the preceding chapter, a number of brands have been successful at getting people to rally around a big idea—and in so doing, have managed to spark a movement that strengthens the relationship between the consumer and the brand, while also helping to bring about some type of change in the culture. Looking at how this has benefited some brands, it's easy to see why a marketer might want to attempt this. But why does the public join in? What are people seeking from this type of enlarged, deepened relationship with a brand or a cause or even just an idea?

In this chapter, we'll explore the motivations and impulses that drive people to join, or in some cases launch, movements of all types. While the previous chapter focused primarily on marketing-driven movements, this chapter features a number of movements that aren't necessarily connected to or supported by any business entity (although there's no reason why they couldn't be in the future; as grassroots movements grow, their needs tend to increase, which creates opportunities for partnering with a like-minded brand, as long as that brand respects and honors the true goals and values of the movement).

I think it's critical that you get a sense of the mindset of movement people if your goal is to attract, connect with, and ultimately collaborate with these people in the future. It should be said at the outset that the people who participate in movements are incredibly diverse—they come from all age groups, ethnicities, incomes, and education levels, you name it. But that's not to say they don't have distinctive qualities and characteristics. At StrawberryFrog, we've made a study of such people, using both formal and highly informal research techniques. We've talked to psychologists and sociologists about this. Mostly, we talk to the people themselves, to find out what it is about a movement that gets them energized, excited, and engaged.

Of course, there's no one reason why people get involved with movements. Guy Kawasaki, whom we met in the previous chapter and who was involved in helping to fan the flames of the early cult movement that developed around Apple, points out, "There are many factors that make people want to rally around a cause or movement. One could be the enchanting nature of the leader of the movement. Another could be that they had a real need for the movement—it enabled them to do things they had always wanted to do and never could do before, so it's changed their lives. Another is just the simple social psychology of wanting to belong to something. Or maybe just wanting to be cool—that's a big factor, too."

FUELED BY RESTLESSNESS

Although there may be any number of reasons why people gravitate toward movements, if you're looking for one central driving force, think in terms of this word: *restlessness*. The derivation of this idea starts with the noted sociologist and social movement expert Neil Smelser, who theorized that social movements (and Smelser was really talking about movements with a capital M, the kind that involve freedom, justice, fairness, and the like) come about because of a combination of factors starting with *social strain*. In the most extreme cases, the strain that Smelser was talking about could take the form of oppression, which, in turn, could spark revolutionary movements and uprisings.

But the more modest movements that are happening all around us, and that are the focus of this book, are more often a response to something slightly less severe than strain. We're talking more about a sense of vague dissatisfaction or restlessness people may have about some aspect of the culture—there's something happening around them that they're not quite content with, and they'd be interested in helping to change it (even if they're not entirely sure how). Going back to Smelser's social movement scenario, as he sees it, the social strain evokes a response in people that becomes a shared belief ("things must change!"). At that point, the movement begins to self-organize and gain momentum.

Regardless of whether they're reacting to large social strains or small stirrings of restlessness, the original group of people who are the first to respond usually forms the core of the movement—these people are what Smelser (and lots of us) calls the "true believers." They will tend to shape the group's identity and its early agenda. They may even develop a distinct language for the movement, which can be expressed in neologistic or repurposed words, powerful symbols, code, or distinctive attire. These semiotics can help separate insiders from outsiders, fostering a community bond. Most important, the true believers will serve as the evangelists of the movement, helping to spread the word and attract others. But what are *they* looking to get out of the experience?

THE HERD INSTINCT

To some extent, people who get involved with movements are responding to a very basic instinct, one that seems to be hardwired in all of us: we want to *belong*. Mark Earls, who has studied the phenomenon of group behavior for his book *Herd*, makes the point that humans are and always have been a "we-species"—we're naturally inclined to form herds and to do various things in groups. We do this for lots of self-interested reasons: the group affords protection, provides strength in numbers, and offers the support and help of fellow group members in solving problems or dealing with difficult challenges.

It all makes sense, and yet the idea that we're highly individualistic tends to dominate in Western culture—and it particularly dominates in marketing and advertising. As Earls points out, the notion of the "we-species" runs counter to the "me-driven" individualism that forms the basis for much of conventional marketing. And as marketing grows ever more targeted, the goal seems to be to somehow isolate and connect with people on a one-to-one basis, giving each person an individualized message designed to persuade that person that it's in his or her individual self-interest to buy Brand X. As Earls indicates, this is, for starters, a nearly impossible marketing task. (How can you possibly customize marketing to please so many disparate, diverse individuals?) In addition, however, this kind of microtargeting may be missing the larger point of what *really* influences people to do the things they do.

Are we truly likely to change our behavior because we get a targeted message from a company we probably don't know or care about? Or are we more likely to adjust our behavior based on what we're seeing, hearing, and learning from the people who are close to us? Earls and many others make a strong case for the latter. We often do what we do in response to the people around us. If you want a stark example of this, Earls suggests looking at what occurs at concerts or sports stadiums when people engage in the activity known as "the wave." It's not caused by external forces; nobody is telling each of those people, on an individual basis, to rise and throw his or her hands in the air at a specific time. It occurs based on interaction between individuals who are in close proximity to one another. Or to put it simply, if the person next to you rises up, you probably will, too.

The point of all this, from a marketing standpoint, is that marketers should be aware that people within a group have a very strong influence on one another. If you can win over some members of the group, there is a good chance that they will carry your message—with more credibility and persuasiveness than any ad—to other members of the group.

BECOMING MORE OF "YOURSELF" WITHIN A MOVEMENT

This does not mean that people who join movements are conformists, or that they tend to lose their individuality when they join movements. More often, the opposite is true. Douglas Atkin, formerly of Meetup.com, who has studied and written about the formation of movements, cults, and online communities, observes that people join these types of groups not to escape themselves, but rather, he says, "to become *more* themselves."

That may seem paradoxical but, as Atkin points out, a community of likeminded enthusiasts can create an environment in which someone may finally feel free to express what he or she believes most strongly (in part because the person is surrounded by others who share and support that point of view). It can also be a place where one's difference from the outside world is seen as a virtue, not a handicap. Within the Apple movement, being a geek who's obsessed with tech specs is cool.

Nor does joining a movement cause someone to be cut off from the rest of the world that exists outside the movement. In fact, what's becoming increasingly clear is that people who engage on one issue are likely to do so on other issues as well. They may belong to multiple movements and online communities that are "porous," in the sense that there is plenty of freedom for members to move in and out easily. In the past, someone might devote his or her life to one cause or movement, but today the threshold for participation and involvement is much lower. One can belong to a dozen different movements—and can choose to broadcast some of those affiliations, while keeping others quiet.

That said, there is a strong sense of community and loyalty that tends to form within movements. This is not news: the power of group loyalty—even among group members who do not have long-standing relationships with one another—was first demonstrated in a landmark study conducted 40 years ago by the psychologist Henri Tajfel. In Tajfel's experiment, strangers were sorted into random groups. Almost immediately, people bonded with fellow group members and actually discriminated against those outside the group. Tajfel's research led to the theory of social identity, which posits that people have an inherent tendency to want to be identified with one or more groups. This is part of the reason why belonging to movements has such strong appeal to so many of us, and why close bonds are formed within those movements.

Part of what makes the bond among members within a movement so strong is a shared sense of purpose. But often, there's also a shared feeling among people inside the movement that they are, in some important way, "different" from those outside the group. In studying movements, we've seen a strong "insiders" versus "outsiders" mentality. People inside the movement may feel, for instance, that they are the only ones who fully understand or appreciate the idea or issue that the movement revolves around; no one else truly "gets it" (and "it" can refer to everything from, say, understanding how truly awesome Apple is to realizing how critical it is to protect the rights of animals).

MOVEMENT GRASSROOTS ANIMAL
ABUSE AWARENESS

EXEMPLAR PATRICK'S MOVEMENT

THE BIG IDEA Give a face to the animal protection movement by championing and broadcasting the dramatic story of Patrick, a rescued pit bull who had been left to die in a garbage can. Patrick's Movement began mobilizing people one by one via Facebook to petition to change their state laws to protect abused animals.

STARTED Rachel Wolf founded the movement in New Jersey in March 2011.

HOW IT SPREAD The shocking story and photos of the starving pit bull named Patrick garnered a lot of initial media coverage. New Jersey resident Rachel Wolf (who adopted Patrick) started an immediately popular Facebook page for Patrick's Law that led people in other states to create their own Facebook pages to encourage awareness and change. There are now more than 100 international Facebook pages for what is now known as Patrick's Movement.

WHERE IT STANDS Coverage of Patrick's recovery continues to buzz around the Internet, and several foundations have been set up in his honor. The movement's blog posts information on how to petition local governments for new laws and set up local rallies held in Patrick's name. The founder of the movement withdrew from leadership after the first three months, yet the state-by-state movement continues to grow and share information via the central Patrick's Movement Facebook page.

QUOTE "As a member of 'Patrick: The National Movement', members are encouraged to no longer hope and wish for animal abuse law reform and increased sentencing for abusers, but lend their voices to achieve it. Public outcry causes change." —Patrick's Movement Facebook page

WEBSITE ThePatrickMovement.blogspot.com; Facebook.com/ PatrickTheNationalMovement

---

This insider/outsider element can be of critical importance when marketers become involved with movements. For example, it clearly helped Apple and Diesel, as discussed in the previous chapter, when they developed "insider" appeal among a core group of true believers who felt they knew more about Apple products and philosophy than others, or who were "in" on the inside joke of Diesel's advertising.

When we worked with one of our early clients, the athletic shoe brand ASICS, on the relaunch of the Japanese-made shoe called the Onitsuka Tiger, we found that members of the movement that formed around this brand, first in Europe and then worldwide, absolutely loved all the inside references to Japanese culture that were contained in our ads—indeed, the more obscure the reference, the more they appreciated it. Likewise, they liked the fact that it wasn't easy to buy a pair of Tiger shoes. You couldn't get them at any old Foot Locker store; you really had to go out of your way to seek them out. That lent an air of in-the-know exclusivity to the product (see the sidebar "Creating a Japanese Cult Craze").

Of course, this whole aspect of insider appeal and exclusivity can be a double-edged sword for marketers: if a brand movement becomes popular enough to go mainstream, there is the risk that the "insiders" may begin to lose their enthusiasm for it once all those "outsiders" have jumped on the bandwagon.

THE DIFFERENCE BETWEEN MOVEMENTS AND TRIBES

I think there's a misconception that movements are like "tribes," to use the term popularized by author Seth Godin and others. But I tend to take issue with using that term in this context because calling a group a tribe suggests that there is homogeneity within the group. Tribes often form around people with the same ethnicity, the same heritage, the same geographic location, and so on. A movement, on the other hand, can be extremely diverse, bringing together all kinds of people, from anywhere and everywhere, as long as they share the fundamental idea or passion that drives the movement.

And while a tribe (like a cult or a clan) tends to have rigid dogma and a closed-off nature, movements are powered by openness, the freedom to belong, and the power of coalition. The diversity of the people within a cultural movement can be one of its great strengths. It means there are more varied skills to draw upon, wider connections, and an ability to cross boundaries and connect with other movements.

From the standpoint of those who might wish to influence or engage with movements, it might be easier if they *were* tribes—if they were, you could focus on winning over the tribal chief. But movements are far more democratic, and influence is spread out within the group. To appeal to movements, you must appeal to the members—by inspiring them or helping them in some way as they try to achieve the movement's purpose.

We studied a variety of movements for this book. Some were aligned with brands and some were not; some involved very serious issues, and others were dedicated more to creative passions or even just fun pursuits. What we discovered is something that people within movements probably already know: that movements right now are attracting people with big ideas, boundless energy, great entrepreneurial and organizational skills, and loads of passion. Here's a brief look at the people behind two rapidly growing movements, one focused on the ways we live, and the other on how we work.

REINVENTING OUR "GOLDEN YEARS": THE AGING IN PLACE MOVEMENT

The leaders of the growing Aging in Place movement, Lois Steinberg and Rob Walden, may never be enshrined in museums or history books along with the leaders of the social justice and civil rights movements. But if you're a person of a certain age, or even if you just know or care about people of a certain age, this is a big and meaningful idea—and one that is rallying people around the country to join forces and take action.

In a nutshell, it's about finding ways to enable senior citizens to live independently in their homes for as long as this is safely possible. For many seniors, it represents a much-desired alternative to being pushed or pressured into leaving their homes and familiar surroundings to go to assisted-living facilities or other types of senior facilities. While those types of facilities are certainly appropriate for some people, they're not for everyone; the Aging in Place movement takes the position that people should have the right to choose—and that we, as a society, should try to make it possible and even practical for some to be able to choose independent living at home.

For an idea like this one to become a movement, people have to act on it—and it usually starts with impassioned leaders. In this case, Rob Walden and Lois Steinberg have emerged as two of the people who've spearheaded this movement through a grassroots New York–based group, Center for Aging in Place. The movement can be traced to Beacon Hill Village in Boston, where a few years ago, a neighborhood initiative sprang up that involved local residents helping to care for and provide help to seniors in the neighborhood who were living at home, on their own. Walden and Steinberg saw an article about Beacon Hill and discussed trying to get something similar started in their own neighborhood. "The concept seemed like it could be replicated throughout the country," Walden says. The idea was to take the knowledge and experience from Beacon Hill to help a second neighborhood, "and then the first two could help the third, and so on." Through online networking, Rob and Lois found a group of social activists in another community who were already working on a similar program. They agreed to provide some help in setting up a larger group.

Next, Rob and Lois spread word of what they were doing among volunteers that they knew; a number of those people brought the idea back to their own neighborhoods, and soon a few additional aging-in-place communities were starting to form. "We also looked for opportunities to speak to any group that wanted to hear about the concept of aging in place, wanted to know what was going on, or needed advice on getting started," Rob says. Gradually a group of core organizers emerged.

The group figured out quickly that it needed to establish a forum for networking. "We called it the 'village council' and met more or less monthly," Walden says. The forum became a way to share strategies and successes. As the movement evolved, groups were formed to tackle ongoing common problems (marketing, fund-raising, PR, sustainability). Board committees were formed, creating a structure not unlike that of a corporation. "It is like creating a small business," says Walden, who works at it full time (he's retired, although he puts that word in quotation marks). What keeps the group growing and moving forward is the energy and passion of people who are committed to the central idea: that seniors should have more of a choice in how they spend their later years, and that, as Steinberg says, we should all have a hand in being able to design the way we'll spend those years.

MOVEMENT   AGING IN PLACE

EXEMPLAR   THE CENTER FOR AGING IN PLACE

THE BIG IDEA   Aging in place is a movement that is national in scope but local in practice, aimed at enhancing the quality of life of aging people by enabling them to remain in their homes as long as this is safely possible. The Center for Aging in Place is a growing local nonprofit that provides resources and services to facilitate community start-up and also facilitates the exchange of ideas among individual communities via its website.

STARTED   Lois Steinberg and Rob Walden started the Center for Aging in Place in Westchester County, New York, in 2008.

HOW IT SPREAD   Information about the center was spread through articles in local publications, word of mouth, and common ground concerning the inevitability that parents grow older and decisions regarding care will eventually need to be made. The Helen Andrus Benedict Foundation has contributed generously, helping with funding and support.

WHERE IT STANDS NOW   So far, the movement is mostly local and volunteer in nature. It is a grassroots movement that people make their own by thinking about their own options for elder care. The Center for AIP currently has ten membership groups in Westchester County.

QUOTE   "Empowering older people to remain in their homes as they age benefits not only them personally but the community at large. Today's generation of seniors is fitter and living longer, and they bring to their communities a wealth of education and experience coupled with the time and talent to lead, serve, and invest." —Lois Steinberg, founder

WEBSITE   CenterforAginginPlace.org

The movement clearly has needs. Part of its mandate is to help provide at-home services for seniors, and it relies heavily on volunteers for that. But Walden acknowledges that there might be a significant role for outside supporters and partners to play— providing space for meetings and events, donating products that seniors need, or arranging for special services. Walden is interested in working with partner companies, but he is wary, as well: "I think companies need to be careful not to just jump in," he says. "It might make it look as if they are trying to co-opt the movement for profit. A more constructive way would be to partner in a way that helps movement participants be successful." He also thinks it would make more sense for a company to get involved with the age in place movement if that business has some kind of track record and positive image with the movement's constituents.

THE CO-WORKING MOVEMENT

While Walden and Steinberg are focused on how and where we live as we age, Ned Dodington, who along with Matthew Wettergreen has launched Caroline Collective, is trying to reinvent the way we work. Specifically, Caroline Collective is a Houston-based initiative that's part of the burgeoning "co-working" movement—an endeavor to create work environments where people from different work backgrounds can come together, sit down, plug in, and (despite not working on the same projects or at the same companies) collaborate in a friendly atmosphere. The movement is an outgrowth of the recognition that in today's changing work environment, there's a need to develop more alternative, shared workspaces and communities.

Dodington says that he and cofounder Wettergreen got involved with the cause almost by happenstance. "We were dreaming and scheming about a kind of artists' space at the same time that 'co-working' started to take off in other cities, like New York,

Philadelphia, and San Francisco. We felt an immediate affinity with the movement." Dodington says the co-working movement is "amazingly inclusive, and we got involved simply by contacting the leaders of the movement in other cities and asking them for guidance and support. Half a year later, we had our own space and an opening party with over 1,200 people in attendance."

Using social media strategies to get the word out in the community, Dodington says he made a point of emphasizing "the public ownership of the event or cause—letting people know that if you help, volunteer, or provide in any way, you will be thanked in a meaningful way, and you will have had a hand in the direction of Caroline Collective. This was a very strong principle that Matthew and I had from the very beginning and that we've defended— that the 'community' as a group is calling the shots and directing Caroline Collective. Matthew and I are merely facilitators." By allowing members "to feel active and empowered to hold their own events, teach classes, and have poetry slams, dance-offs, movie nights, and business development classes on their own as a part of the collective, it means there is a constant buzz of something going on. Which shows that the movement is in fact moving—it has a life and energy of its own."

MOVEMENT CO-WORKING

EXEMPLAR CAROLINE COLLECTIVE

THE BIG IDEA Caroline Collective is a showcase for the co-working movement, offering a private workspace, public art space, open desk space, and a robust website spreading the word about the benefits of collective workspace environments. These kinds of settings give participants the option of concentrating privately or collaborating with others to expand their ideas, network, and socialize.

STARTED Ned Dodington and Matthew Wettergreen founded Caroline Collective in Houston, Texas, in 2008.

HOW IT SPREAD Local press and basic word of mouth helped Caroline Collective grow into a successful institution made up of entrepreneurs, salespeople, bloggers, engineers, artists, musicians, nonprofits, and programmers. Now local businesses tap into these influentials to help build buzz around events and launches.

WHERE IT STANDS NOW There are more than 40 active members. "Over the past three years, there have been hundreds, if not thousands, of people who have come through our doors, lent a hand, or contributed in some way," says founder Ned Dodington.

QUOTE "It's inevitable that we'll see more co-working in the coming years. Not only is it reflective of a cultural and psychic shift in the workplace, but it is also a very feasible and sensible way for many people to optimize their workday to fit their complex daily schedules. It simply makes too much sense for it not to become the new norm." —Ned Dodington, founder

WEBSITE Carolinecollective.cc

Like Walden and Steinberg, Dodington and Wettergreen put long hours and considerable energy into the movement: "Sometimes it's frustrating, and there are moments when it feels completely out of control," Dodington says. "There's a lot of 'embrace the chaos.' But when it's working, it's also quite a rush."

MOTIVATION 3.0:
THE HUNGER FOR PURPOSE

What's interesting is that a lot of people we've encountered who are involved in movements are devoting tremendous amounts of energy to building a shared endeavor, even though the prospects of any real financial gain are limited or nil.

I have no proof of it, but I suspect this may be connected to a growing social phenomenon that the author Daniel Pink has referred to as "motivation 3.0," the idea being that what is really driving more and more people these days has less to do with financial incentives than with finding a sense of belonging and purpose.

I spoke to Pink about this, and he said the rise of movements does seem to be connected to this growing hunger for a sense of meaningful purpose. "People want to make a contribution," Pink says. "They want what they do to matter and have an impact on the world. When people are part of a movement, and feel that sense of contribution, it's incredibly satisfying—and it motivates them to do more."

In addition, Pink says, "there's lots of research that shows people are motivated by making progress. So if they're somehow moving forward, or if the cause itself is advancing, that can provide a motivational jolt. If you think about it, the very word *movement* suggests the idea of growing, evolving, moving forward. Human beings want to progress; it's part of who we are."

Along with wanting to solve problems and contribute to the world around them, a lot of people seem to be joining movements as a means of creative self-expression. The growing and multistreamed "craft" movement, along with the related DIY (do-it-yourself) movement, actually ties together lots of mini-movements, all of them having to do with making (or fixing up) your own stuff, instead of relying on corporations to make it for you. A leader within this overall movement is Faythe Levine (see sidebar), whose fiercely independent attitudes reflect the kind of spirit one encounters throughout the craft/DIY phenomenon. What Levine and her ilk have been working to build is a new world in which anyone can be a "manufacturer"—and in which the best ideas compete in a wide-open marketplace.

To bring about this kind of change, a coordinated and collective effort is needed—people must join together to engage in what the writer Clay Shirky refers to as a "shared endeavor." Shirky believes that for various reasons, having to do with sociological shifts, technology, and other factors, we're seeing an increase in these shared endeavors (which I would call movements) as people come together to try to take on challenges and create new opportunities. The examples abound: Charity: Water is a shared endeavor aimed at helping people around the world get water; TOMS Shoes is an entrepreneurial movement aimed at selling shoes while also providing free shoes to kids in need; InnoCentive brings together inventors and innovators to try to solve complex technical problems; Kickstarter is a movement that provides grassroots funding for worthwhile projects; Wikipedia could be thought of as a shared endeavor and also a movement, as it brings people together for the purpose of creating a self-generated encyclopedia of and by the people.

Wherever you look these days, people are forming movements to try to solve a problem or address something that is needed in the culture. In our research, we found examples of movements that started as a response to a very specific problem that affected one person, but quickly expanded into a movement because the problem was relevant to many other people. Angela Daffon started a movement called Jodi's Voice in response to the murder of her friend and neighbor Jodi Sanderholm, who was the victim of a stalker. What started as one woman's attempt to advocate on behalf of antistalking laws has now become a gathering point for victims to exchange stories, support one another, and continue to work toward more public education and tougher legislation with regard to this problem. Similarly, we've encountered folks who've lost jobs and then started movements aimed at others who are in the same predicament; parents and students who've had enough of bullying in school and launched movements to try to stop it; and drivers who are fed up with seeing other drivers yakking on cell phones and started movements to curtail it.

The bottom line is that there are people out there who want, as perhaps never before, to solve problems, to express themselves, to create, to innovate, to advocate, and to collaborate. They find that they can't change the world all by themselves—they need the power of a movement to do it.

The question is, do these people need or want anything from the world of business? Is there a proper role for business in this purpose-driven, movement-oriented environment?

In our conversations with people who've started a variety of movements, we raised this question and found that the response was positive—but also cautious. Movement leaders such as Levine, Dodington, and Walden point out that there's plenty of room for businesses to get involved with movements on a supportive level. But there is also concern that companies might seek to co-opt movements—that they might try to attach themselves to a cause or issue that they don't really believe in or care about, just to get some PR value out of it.

So a theme we'll be coming back to repeatedly in the chapters ahead is authenticity. As we've seen in this chapter, people who are involved in movements are passionate and care deeply about the issues that are at the heart of the movement, and they can sniff out those who don't share their interests or commitment. If you align with an existing movement or try to spark a new movement, you need to recognize that this is serious stuff. Don't take up a cause unless you really aim to do something constructive and helpful on behalf of the people who care about that cause. And you need to understand that the people on the ground, the ones who actually power the movement, are ultimately the ones in charge.

That said, movements provide great opportunities to engage with people on a positive, creative, supportive level. To get a sense of what movements need from business, let's return to Neal Smelser and his theories on social movements, which provide clues to possible ways in which businesses can help spark or in some way encourage and support all types of movements. As I mentioned earlier, Smelser believes that the movement phenomenon starts with social strain, but that there are other conditions and factors that, when present, can enable people to respond to social strain by starting a movement. Smelser cited such factors as *conduciveness*, referring to conditions that might make it easy for people to join together around an idea (in the past, this often had to do with the proximity of members to one another). He also pointed to the formation of *generalized belief*, wherein a group of people begins to share an attitude or understanding. And he cited the need for *mobilization*, the stage at which people begin to organize and take action.

Conduciveness is actually less of a factor today than it was in the past; in today's superconnected digital environment (as we'll see in Chapter 4), almost any situation anywhere can be conducive to a movement. We're all connected now, so proximity is simply not as big an issue as it once was.

But there's still a need to give voice to and clearly articulate the big idea—or, in Smelser's term, the generalized belief—that people can share and rally around. That alternative idea must come to the fore somehow, but where does it come from? It can come from an individual like Faythe Levine, who models, and becomes the champion of, a new way of doing things. It can emerge from a group of people, who may be acting together or separately. It can be sparked by the introduction of a new technology or a product (case in point: Nintendo's Wii system, as discussed in the previous chapter). But it can also come from a company that introduces a compelling new way of thinking about a technology, a product, a social problem, or a way of behaving. How an idea like that is expressed—particularly in terms of the language, imagery, and semiotics used—can be the key to whether it captures the imagination of enough people with enough passion to launch a movement. In addition to helping to articulate the big idea, a company can also play a role in the mobilization stage by providing ways for people to begin to take action on the idea.

WHAT YOU CAN PROVIDE FOR MOVEMENT PEOPLE (AND WHAT YOU CAN'T)

In other words, the passion is already out there—it's burning in people like Walden, Dodington, Levine, and countless others. What's needed are big ideas, platforms, and outlets for all of that passion. With a grateful nod to Smelser's theories, I think it all breaks down as follows: for a movement to happen, you need to tap into the passion, energy, or restlessness that people have concerning some aspect of the culture. To do this, you need to articulate a big idea that somehow addresses the restlessness and is expressed in a fresh, compelling way (which is where semiotics can come into play). If you succeed in doing that, you may end up with a group of true believers who are ready to act—and at that point, you can foster that action by providing support, tools, and platforms.

So you end up with a formula that looks something like this:

Restlessness + alternative idea (expressed through semiotics) + true believers + facilitation = a cultural movement

A brand or organization that's looking to spark a movement really can't control the first and third factors. That restless dissatisfaction is already out there; as for the true believers, either they will rally around an idea or they won't. But there is plenty of opportunity to shape or help express the alternative idea itself. In the next two chapters, we'll talk at length about finding that big idea, shaping it, and expressing it in a way that can inspire people to gather around it. We'll also cover the critical concept of facilitation, which generally involves finding ways to help those true believers to connect with one another, share information, collaborate, and take purposeful action.

It has never been easier to provide that facilitation than it is right now. Because of digital technology and the social media revolution, you can connect with people—and, in turn, help them connect with one another—in ways that were never possible before. Next up, we'll look at how digital connectivity is proving to be a central factor in the current rise of movements. For that reason and a couple of others we'll examine in that chapter, it has never before been as feasible as it is now to spark a movement, to foster its growth, and to increase its impact on the world.

ON THE FRONT LINES OF THE CRAFT MOVEMENT WITH FAYTHE LEVINE

Faythe Levine has emerged as one of the leaders of the DIY/craft movement. She's the founder of Art vs. Craft, a well-known indie craft fair, and her signature piece and most successful craft project, the Messenger Owl, a hand-cut and machine-sewn plush owl, after being featured on HGTV, became so popular that Levine couldn't keep up with the demand. In 2008, Levine produced and directed the documentary film *Handmade Nation: The Rise of DIY, Art, Craft, and Design*.

Why and how did you get involved with the DIY craft movement?

I never had any specific intention to be involved or associated with a movement. It was about finding community and connecting with like-minded productive and creative individuals. My initial contact with the DIY punk community came when I was 14, through music and 'zine culture. When I started using the Internet to connect with other makers around 2001, having this ability to connect with people regardless of location definitely was a turning point for me. As I established my online presence, my reach and understanding of what was going on "around me" was growing. This allowed me to generate excitement for larger projects more easily.

Can you talk about the motivations of people in this movement, and also the ways these people interact with one another?

Well, the interesting thing about the DIY community is that it's not made up of a specific type of person. There are threads that tie people together. The act of making and producing things and having a creative drive would be the main ones. But on top of that, I think there is a political motivation for some people. There is a feeling of empowerment you get when you realize that you have the control and ability to make something and take that thing and possibly sell it. There's a really idealistic idea of wanting to be a working artist and wanting to survive as a working artist.

As far as how people interact, one of the ongoing topics of discussion during interviews for my documentary *Handmade Nation* was the amount of noncompetitiveness between makers. This included skill sharing, material sourcing, process, and positive feedback by those who identified with and participated in the community. These interviews were conducted primarily in 2006, and I do believe there have been some major shifts since then, not exclusive to, but fueled by, major corporations and larger established design-ers lifting or ripping off independent designers and makers, result-ing in mass production of work that wasn't theirs to reproduce.

Is being part of a movement like this hard work—and is it satisfying?

I believe that the most satisfying work is always the hardest. Orga-nizing projects, people, and happenings with the intention of mak-ing something has been my motivation since I realized I had the ability to inspire people to do something with their life. Even if this something is just learning to sew a button on a shirt for the first time, the feeling people get from working with their hands can provide the empowerment to create much larger and more powerful things.

What helps a movement draw attention?

What seemed to draw the most attention to handmade was the rise in popularity of the aesthetic within mainstream culture. But I believe there were many factors, including the "green" aware-ness trend, Etsy.com, and of course the ability to share information about one another's work via social networking sites. The popular-ity of blogging and online media has allowed those who might have never come across certain work to stumble or click on it or inten-tionally read articles or shop with those they wouldn't otherwise have access to.

What do you think of companies getting involved with move-ments—what role can they play that would be most constructive? What should they not do?

I believe that talking about "companies" is too vague, and that in the end a case-by-case study of company involvement would be necessary to answer this question. But I will say that I have mixed emotions about the involvement of companies within movements. Obviously monetary assistance and support are often needed by creatives; however, having a corporate hand in the mix can squelch the essence of the driving force behind what's happening. What a company should never do is assume it can buy a feeling that is generated by people.

CREATING A JAPANESE CULT CRAZE

How do you take an outdated athletic shoe brand and give it new life? One way is to create a cultural movement rooted in some of the unique heritage of the brand. ASICS was an authentic, unconventional "cult" brand that used to be worn by Bruce Lee. That connection had been lost over the years, but StrawberryFrog wanted to bring back some of that authentic cult feeling. The company's Onitsuka Tiger line was made in Japan, but we flipped that idea so that the campaign was all about "made *of* Japan"—all kinds of interesting bits of Japanese retro culture were brought to life and shared with the community. The movement was built around people in Europe, the United States, and elsewhere who wanted to take part in that culture, who wanted to share it and live it.

The semiotics of the campaign revolved around iconic 1960s-style Japanese action heroes. Picking up the theme, a short film was produced about following one's dream, entitled "Fish Gutter"; it ended up in 50 film festivals and reached 250,000 members of the influential art house crowd. (The film told the story of a Japanese fish factory worker training for an Olympic marathon—which he intended to run on his hands, wearing tiny Tiger sneakers.) The film caught on online and reached another million people. We also created a hundred pieces of Japanese manga art, featuring Tiger shoes, and distributed the artwork to bars, music venues, and other trendy spots.

Perhaps the most popular thing we did—it drew the attention of 5 million people online—was to create the world's first legal performance-enhancing drug, made available just prior to the Olympics, courtesy of Onitsuka Tiger. It was called Hero Breath because that's what it was—cans were filled with the actual breath of Japanese gold medalists from the 1964 Olympics. As the movement grew, people passionately collected and swapped the manga art, the posters of Japanese superhero bears, and the cans of Hero Breath. We never really went mass market with this campaign because we didn't have to: once the movement got going, people sought out these Japanese culture artifacts, and they sought out the shoes as well. Sales of ASICS jumped 300 percent above forecast.

CHAPTER 4

Why Movements Are Suddenly Becoming . . . a Movement

"Advice to the youth of Egypt: Put vinegar or onion under your scarf for tear gas." That message, posted on Facebook during the height of the Egyptian uprising in early 2011, came from protesters in nearby Tunisia, who had previously toppled their own government and now had some practical tips to share with the rebels in neighboring Egypt.

As the *New York Times* reported, the Tunisian and Egyptian protesters had been using Facebook and other social media to communicate with one another for months before the Egyptian uprising. Relying on digital connectivity, they created a movement that crossed national boundaries and joined together people who, in many cases, had never met, but who shared the same dream of spreading democracy through the Arab world. The members of this pan-Arab youth movement used Facebook to trade notes on the practical tactics of nonviolence. They also used Internet search engines to educate themselves on these tactics, drawing lessons from earlier movements around the world.

One Facebook group that was set up by protesters was named "We Are All Khalid Said," a tribute to a young Egyptian who'd been killed by police. The website stirred passions by showing clips of police violence. In the days leading up to one of the major protests in Tahrir Square, the site was used to mobilize support, in hopes of generating a turnout of 50,000. It got more than 100,000 people to commit. And at the actual rally, people shouted slogans they'd read on Facebook.

If there was any doubt that social media could change the world, that doubt was erased during the Mideast uprisings (and again, more recently, in the Occupy Wall Street movement, which used Facebook and Twitter to generate momentum and then build upon it). But in the same way that technology made it possible for people in Tunisia or New York to quickly share big ideas and mobilize masses to take action, it is also having that effect on "movements with a small m" by making it possible for anyone, anywhere, to build momentum for an endeavor or a cause.

It comes down to this: technology is enabling people to connect with one another as never before. In the past, you needed to somehow bring many like-minded people together in one place—with the public square often serving as that place—in order for your movement to actually exist. Now, the movement can come to life in cyberspace, and if there is still a need to gather people in the square (as there sometimes is, even today), the Internet serves as an ideal organizing tool.

Soon it will be hard to remember this, but once upon a time, people had to hand out leaflets on the street. They had to go person to person to spread the word about a movement. Often, the transformation that occurred in an uprising would happen in a physical gathering place, such as on the street or in the public square; that was where, as author Steven Pinker has noted, private knowledge would become public knowledge. And it could take a while.

For comparison's sake, think about how past movements (encompassing everything from social to political to religious movements) tended to spread from one person to another before we were all so interconnected. Judaism, for example, achieved its early growth as a religious movement by spreading the word hand to hand. Similarly, dissident activity in the old Soviet bloc was often advanced by the practice known as *samizdat*, which involved the underground printing of documents that were then handed from one person to the next. Building a movement using these methods was a long and difficult process.

In general, it's always been hard to organize and mobilize large groups of people to take action, as the author Clay Shirky points out in his book *Here Comes Everybody*. Shirky notes that part of what made collective action difficult in the past was the sheer complexities of coordination and communication within a group, particularly a large one: how do you get everyone on the same page at the same time?

GETTING EVERYONE
ON THE SAME PAGE

Practically overnight, the Internet and the rise of social networking media pretty much wiped out this problem. Technology made it relatively simple to share information quickly with many people simultaneously, and then to update that information constantly—meaning that everybody really *could* be on the same page at the same time. Or to think of it another way, you didn't have to physically gather in the public square to share the latest developments and rally the crowd; the public square now existed online, where one could easily organize activities and mobilize forces. And being the open, collaborative medium that it is, the web also, as Shirky points out, lends itself to a different kind of movement—one that tends to be less dependent on leaders, with more shared responsibilities among members. This generally will allow a movement to advance much more quickly because group effort usually trumps individual effort.

The bottom line is that "technology has opened up new—and more—options for creating a movement and engaging in one," observes Dr. Kathleen Gerson, professor of sociology at New York University. "The Internet provides an opportunity for social networking, communicating, and organizing. It has facilitated communication across time and space at little to no cost. People of various political persuasions and with specific interests in various issues and political persuasions can now find each other and get together—without having to meet face-to-face."

Gerson says that this phenomenon has a big impact on the formation of smaller, niche movements. "Even if a group is focusing on very specific issues with limited appeal, it's easier to find others who share its concerns and to develop low-cost ways of organizing," she says. "This access spans people across the political spectrum and helps people from the right to the left to organize without having to go through, or rely on the resources of, structured parties. And people who don't see themselves as political but who care about social issues can now pursue similar avenues. So it is likely that we are seeing a period of expanding diversity as varied groups mobilize on a wide array of issues."

The sociologist Saskia Sassen of Columbia University observes that in the past, if you wanted to "be part of a group or to change the world," you pretty much were limited to joining established cultural or political organizations. "But today there is a far wider range of options," she says. You can join small fringe groups or, better yet, start your own. And, as she points out, you can quickly go global, because the web is global. All of this helps explain why, to put it succinctly, movements have become a movement.

This increased capacity to work together toward shared goals should, in theory, mean that we can begin to innovate more, create more, and solve more of our problems as a society. It's still too early to say whether all that will pan out, but certainly the potential is there. We're seeing, for example, that it is becoming more feasible now for activists to use new technology to quickly organize and mobilize movements aimed at tackling some of our thorniest social problems. An initiative such as Charity: Water—Scott Harrison's grassroots movement to try to build wells, pumps, and other water delivery systems in parched areas around the world—has quickly gained widespread exposure and popular support, primarily via Harrison's savvy use of the web and social media. The same is true for a movement like Architecture for Humanity, which brings together designers and architects to rebuild housing in areas that have been struck by natural disasters. The group's founder, Cameron Sinclair, relies on digital technology to do everything from soliciting design ideas to raising funds.

We're now even seeing movements that are designed to encourage and support other movements, largely by employing the tools of digital connectivity. The group Movements.org, cofounded by Google veteran Jason Liebman, provides "a support network for grassroots activists using digital tools," according to Liebman. The group works with social activists, nongovernmental organizations (NGOs), and governments to show them how to use social media to be more effective in trying to solve problems, and it recently launched an online hub where activists can connect with each other and access resources, including tips on using Google and Facebook to advance activism efforts more quickly and efficiently.

Another new group, Purpose.com, is "attempting to deploy the collective power of millions of citizens and consumers to help solve some of the world's biggest problems." The group was born out of successful experiments in mass digital participation, including the creation of Avaaz, an online political movement that has attracted 9 million members worldwide. Now the group is partnering with movements aimed at fighting cancer, eliminating nuclear weapons, and supporting gay rights. Jeremy Heimans, the group's founder, maintains that through the savvy use of digital technology—and with a simple, compelling message—it's now possible to build momentum behind causes without having huge amounts of resources. "If you give people something compelling enough, they'll want to tell their friends to do the same. You don't need expensive media or lobbying efforts when you create efforts that make people *want* to take action."

Among the digerati, there is great optimism that in our increasingly connected society, we'll be able to rally the public to do things that government or business cannot achieve. *Wired* magazine recently declared that the rise of social media represents "the vanguard of a larger cultural movement" that the magazine dubbed "The New Socialism." The writer of the piece, Kevin Kelly, explained that this didn't mean that everything would be run by the state; that was the "old socialism." In the new one, people powered by technology are calling the shots. And Kelly predicted that increasingly, they will share information, cooperate, collaborate, and engage in collective efforts to take on daunting challenges.

MOVEMENT PLAYGROUND SAFETY

EXEMPLAR KABOOM!

THE BIG IDEA Playgrounds should be safe and available for children to access in low-income neighborhoods. The inspiration for this movement came when founder Darrell Hammond had learned of two children who had suffocated to death while playing in an abandoned car because they lacked a proper, safe place to play. Once the KaBOOM! planning is done (with a lot of input from local kids and adults), the actual building of the playground happens in just one day.

STARTED Darrell Hammond and Dawn Hutchison founded KaBOOM! in Washington, D.C., in 1996.

HOW IT SPREAD The "Let Us Play" campaign worked to increase safety through the renovation of preexisting community playgrounds. KaBOOM! also has partnerships with local businesses and corporate backing from companies like Home Depot. Both Laura Bush and Michelle Obama have been involved with spreading the word about KaBOOM!'s efforts. The group teamed up with famed architect David Rockwell to form the Playful City USA program in 2007. Social media keeps KaBOOM! and its volunteers and members up-to-date. The movement also offers a self-organized community and tool kit online, with step-by-step ways in which communities can successfully manage their own projects.

WHERE IT STANDS NOW In its fifteenth year, KaBOOM! funded and built its two-thousandth playground. It has raised more than $200 million and has had an impact on 5.5 million kids with over a million volunteers. In 2011, founder Darrell Hammond published the well-reviewed book *KaBOOM!: How One Man Built a Movement to Save Play*.

QUOTE "We built more than 200 playgrounds last year, but we got more than 14,000 requests. [The problem] is bigger than the resources KaBOOM! has to solve it. And that's why we're trying to crowd-source the solution to get it to be higher on parents', teachers', and administrators' agendas, but also recognizing that if we sense an urgency, there's also a solution that comes behind it." —Darrell Hammond, founder

WEBSITE Kaboom.org

Clay Shirky espouses a similarly optimistic view in his book *Cognitive Surplus*. He points out that in the postindustrial world of the past half century, people gained more free time, but spent a lot of it watching TV. However, the Internet, he argues, is more likely to put that free time to good, productive use. Because it's a medium that connects people instead of cutting them off from each other, and because it enables people to actively engage, participate, and create, Shirky thinks it will result in shared endeavors that produce constructive results—with an early example of this being the creation of Wikipedia.

BUT WHAT DOES ALL THIS HAVE TO DO WITH BUSINESS?

This is a legitimate question, since we tend to separate social issues from business ones—or, at least, we did in the past. But increasingly, business and social issues are coming together. The problems that social activists are focused on (take environmentalism, for example) are now seen as concerns that business can no longer afford to ignore. As customers begin to care deeply about issues, business must care about them, too. If the public is moving toward a world of greater collaboration and sharing, then business must begin to do likewise—or else risk falling out of touch. And if people, newly empowered by technology, are gravitating toward constructive and creative movements, then business needs to figure out what role it can play in this new paradigm.

This may make it sound as if I'm casting business in a reactionary role—that is, something big is happening in the outside world, and companies must, if only for appearances' sake, try to keep up and play along. But actually, I see this whole development as a huge opportunity for business to lead. Because of the digital revolution and the rise of movements, we're in a position to change the way we do business, and particularly the way we market, for the better.

Because of social media, we can connect with our customers better, and more deeply, than we ever could before. We can get a better understanding of what issues concern them, and of some of the ways they may be looking to improve their lives and the world around them. And then we can use our resources—the same resources that we have traditionally used to bombard people with unwanted messages—to help address some of these concerns, dreams, and needs. If that sounds optimistic, absolutely, it is. In the same way that Kelly and Shirky see the possibilities that this new digital landscape will bring out the best in people, I think the new connectivity could bring out the best in marketers by helping us get beyond interrupting and badgering people, to the point where we might actually be contributing something to the mix.

To do that, we need to do some things differently. It starts with recognizing that the old Voice of God model—where we're basically talking down to people, trying to tell them what they should care about—is dead. And I say, good riddance to it. I always thought it was arrogant for marketers, or anyone, to believe they could tell us all what we should be thinking or how we should be living our lives. An important distinction with this new model of movement marketing is that, if it is to be done right, it should be based more on listening than on dictating; it should be based on what people are already thinking about, as opposed to being manufactured out of whole cloth by a couple of clever ad guys.

Digital technology and social networking allow us, as marketers, to be part of the larger conversation if we choose to listen and participate. We shouldn't be trying to hijack that conversation; in effect, that's what we did with traditional advertising, but it won't work in this medium because the people are in charge. What we *can* do is contribute something to the conversation that is actually helpful or useful to people. We can add something to the mix that is good enough, and relevant enough, that people actually may want to react to it, engage with it, and share it with others. When that happens, people become our "media," and they don't just carry a message for us, they actually begin to shape and create the content as they are helping to spread it around.

THE SWARM EFFECT

It's useful to think of this in terms of a swarm metaphor, because movements—particularly those fueled by today's social media—tend to behave the way a swarm of insects does. A swarm moves in one direction as a group, and although it has no leader, it is capable of changing directions quickly to avoid a threat or pursue an opportunity. So how do the individual members of the swarm know when to change direction?

Scientists who study "swarm intelligence" have found that the group is able to share information instantly, based on tiny individual interactions—for example, the antennae of two insects touching for a second—that allow members to guide each other as to what to do next. The swarm is also very good at spotting things (such as food) because there are so many eyes involved. This combination of being adept at picking up on cues all around and being able to share that information quickly enables the swarm to be highly productive and move with great purpose and momentum.

`MOVEMENT`　MAKING SCIENCE COOL

EXEMPLAR　FIRST (FOR INSPIRATION AND RECOGNITION OF SCIENCE AND TECHNOLOGY)

THE BIG IDEA　The goal of FIRST is to encourage students to pursue careers in science and technology through robotics competitions. America has done an excellent job of supporting and promoting achievement in athletics and entertainment. But the future belongs to innovators, and the culture must equally celebrate inventors, researchers, engineers, and scientists in order to inspire children and their teachers to lead the United States into the future.

STARTED　Dean Kamen founded FIRST in 1989.

HOW IT SPREAD　Dean Kamen, the inventor of the Segway and many other products, turned himself into a science evangelist, setting up a dedicated website and giving many interviews on the topic over 20 years. He created a network of mentors and volunteers to recruit and support competition participants. In the early years (and continuing), FIRST also lined up the support of many iconic corporations, who saw their future leaders and workers coming out of the FIRST program.

WHERE IT STANDS NOW　Since the first robotics competition in a gym in Manchester, New Hampshire, FIRST has grown into an international phenomenon with tens of thousands of participants. Hundreds of thousands of competition alumni fill the ranks of tech and engineering businesses. FIRST's new push is to garner the attention and influence of media and popular culture. In summer 2011, FIRST teamed up with entertainer and education supporter will.i.am for a science and robotics special on ABC-TV, which featured a surprise visit by President Obama.

QUOTE "You have teenagers thinking they're going to make millions as NBA stars when that's not realistic for even 1 percent of them. Becoming a scientist or engineer is." —Dean Kamen, founder

WEBSITE UsFirst.org

With regard to people and movements, you could say that social media is now serving as our antennae—it's what is enabling members of a group to quickly pick up and pass around information that can guide the behavior of the group. This could involve everything from sharing survival strategies (this is what worked in Tunisia and in Egypt; let's see if it works on Wall Street) to just sharing favorite YouTube videos. In any case, all the members of the group are out there looking for relevant stuff, and when they find it, they quickly share it with the group—at which point the thing (whatever it is) becomes quite popular overnight.

This type of swarm behavior among humans has important ramifications for marketers. One thing it does is upend the traditional marketing notion that it's important to target messages to "influential" people, who, supposedly, are the leaders and tastemakers that the crowd follows. But if, thanks to social media, today's crowds are actually behaving more like swarms, then this means that the influencers are spread throughout the group—anybody with antennae connected to somebody else's antennae can be an influencer. According to Guy Kawasaki, "this change has turned marketing upside down" because "the old trickle-down, top-down theory of marketing" no longer makes sense if people have come to rely more on the opinions of their tribe than on experts and trendsetters. In this upside-down world, the masses are apt to descend suddenly upon an idea, a cause, or a product—at which point, Kawasaki writes, "the influentials have to pay attention to it or risk looking clueless." The bottom line is that now, Kawasaki says, marketers must begin to "embrace the nobodies."

One more thing to keep in mind about movements and swarms: both tend to move with a sense of purpose. Just as you wouldn't want to get in the way of a swarm, you don't want to get caught standing between a movement and its goal or purpose. But if you can somehow, in some way, help the group to move toward that purpose, you may be able to move with it and reap the benefits of its momentum.

IT TAKES A VILLAGE . . .

An interesting example of this was something StrawberryFrog did recently for Pampers diapers, one of Procter & Gamble's brands. This is the kind of product that represents a challenge in terms of trying to do innovative marketing. A diaper is not the most exciting product in the world, and traditionally this product has been marketed through endlessly repetitive warm-and-fuzzy TV commercials. So how do you build something resembling a movement around diapers? (Please: no bowel movement jokes.)

For us, it started with using social media to listen to young moms so that we could get a sense of what they were concerned about these days. One of the interesting insights was that, in this age of information, mothers (and moms-to-be) are besieged with all kinds of worrisome stories and data: about unhealthy food, lead-based paint, or whatever the crisis of the moment might be.

Mothers needed an online place of refuge, so we created a virtual community that celebrates parenthood and focuses on useful tips—available in the cloud and on all devices such as mobiles, tablets, and computers. Say hello to Pampers Village.

We wanted to make it a place where harried moms would feel welcome, appreciated, and connected to other moms. So we created an online hub that included a reference section for new parents, an entertainment channel called Pampers Theater, a talk show series with advice for new parents, and even a reality show called "Welcome to Parenthood." We didn't shy away from presenting medical information, but we made sure it was presented in a way that was less clinical (and less alarming), with more of a focus on providing practical and accessible advice.

One of the things we wanted to do was create content that people would actually want to take away from the village and share with others. We were able to do this through the creation of apps that were designed to be useful, but also fun. For instance, there was our Hello Baby iPad app (one of the first apps available as the iPad was being launched), a visual pregnancy calendar. The idea was simple, but the technology made it striking: by programming her due date, an expecting mother could get an idea, at any given time, of the actual size of her baby in the womb. The app also provided detailed information about what was happening physically at that stage, but the real impact was visual—a mom could hold the iPad in front of her stomach and see a representation of the baby, in a richly detailed image. Hello Baby quickly became the number one health and fitness app for the iPad—which, in turn, helped bring more mothers to the village. This reinforces my earlier point: if you can find a way to give people something useful, something they can share, they will help to build the movement for you. It also had a particular appeal for dads, giving them another way to share in the experience. In this case, Hello Baby captured new parents at conception instead of nine months later.

CO-CREATION OF CONTENT

I mentioned before that one of the goals of movement marketing is to have people not only share the content you create, but actually be involved in creating that content. When we created the "Against Dumb" movement for Smart Car, we knew that one way to get consumers really invested in the movement was to give them a platform where they could talk about all the things they considered to be examples of overconsumption or just plain dumb consumption. So we used social media to encourage people to "Share Your Dumb" on Facebook. We asked them to submit online photos of the dumbest things they'd ever bought; through online voting, members of the community would select the dumbest of the dumb, with the winner being offered a free Smart Car. The images that people sent in—of absurd products like the sushi stapler and the radio hat—proved to be some of the most interesting and viral content we could've hoped for.

The point is that if you give people a platform and the tools to tell their own stories, you can end up with something that is far more interesting—and more relevant to other members of the movement—than anything you might be able to dream up. This certainly proved to be the case when we launched a movement for Pepsico's True North snacks brand by asking the public to share stories about what serves as their own "true north"—the passionate project or dream they've dedicated their lives to pursuing (see the sidebar "A Movement to the True North").

One of the brand movements of the past few years that I really admire is TOMS Shoes, the company started by entrepreneur Blake Mycoskie with a business plan that called for giving away one pair of shoes for every pair sold. One brilliant thing Mycoskie did was to really make his customers feel that they were an integral part of the endeavor to get free shoes to kids around the world who needed them. In various ways, Mycoskie has shared the uplifting experience of giving away shoes to kids with the members of the TOMS community. The giveaways, which have taken place in impoverished areas in South America, Africa, and elsewhere, are usually filmed or documented in some way, then shared on Facebook, where Mycoskie also maintains steady contact with members of the TOMS movement through his personal blog.

MOVEMENT ## SOCIAL ENTREPRENEURSHIP

EXEMPLAR   ONE FOR ONE MOVEMENT/TOMS SHOES

THE BIG IDEA   The unique business model of *buying one product, giving one product* started as an affordable way to put shoes on the feet of underprivileged children around the world. For every pair of TOMS Shoes purchased, a pair of new shoes is given to a child who needs them. The name "TOMS" refers to "tomorrows."

STARTED   Blake Mycoskie founded TOMS Shoes in 2006.

HOW IT SPREAD The movement spread through media coverage of shoe drops into needy countries, celebrity endorsements, a 2009 Vagabond Tour to reach college campuses in the United States, charities, and receptions to inform the curious, celebrate the supporters, and aid in fund-raising. Founder Blake Mycoskie had some TV cred as a past star of a reality TV show. In spring 2009, Mycoskie's face and organization were the stars of a national AT&T ad campaign.

WHERE IT STANDS NOW As of September 2010, more than 1 million pairs of new shoes had been provided to children in need around the world. The organization has started up One for One Eyewear, a sunglasses/eyeglasses donation arm. Mycoskie published *Start Something That Matters*, a book about passionate entrepreneurship, in September 2011.

QUOTE "If you just go out and try to make money by starting a business, you're going to come up with something that's just like what everyone else has done. But if you look at the world and see opportunities that can be taken more seriously, then you come up with a great idea." —Blake Mycoskie

WEBSITE toms.com

The company has also created mini-movements within the overall movement. For example, TOMS does an annual "One Day Without Shoes" event, during which Mycoskie uses his Facebook forum to rally followers to give up wearing shoes for a day as a means of raising people's awareness of kids around the world who do not have shoes. Through the effective use of social media, combined with a deep sense of shared purpose that Mycoskie has skillfully fostered, TOMS has been able to build the kind of emotional bond with customers that most brands can only dream about. (Would your customers stop wearing shoes for you?) And one of the great benefits of this for the company is that TOMS hasn't had to spend a lot of money on TV commercials. The success of the movement and the compelling, purposeful nature of what Mycoskie is doing have generated extensive media coverage and great word of mouth.

THIS PURPOSEFUL MOMENT IN WHICH WE'RE LIVING

It's pretty clear that digital technology has been a driving force behind the recent rise of movements such as TOMS Shoes. But are there other reasons why people seem to be gravitating toward causes and initiatives such as this one? One could say that the impulse to start and join movements has always been there, and that all that was needed to put it into action was connectivity.

But there may be other factors contributing to the current rise of movements. Bob Johansen of the Institute for the Future, an esteemed think tank that studies trends and provides forecasts of what's coming and where we're headed, believes that these are particularly turbulent times, characterized by what Johansen refers to as VUCA—volatility, uncertainty, complexity, and ambiguity. As Johansen sees it, we're in a period of extreme challenge, with our natural, organizational, and social systems reaching disruptive tipping points. And he notes that as people try to cope with so much complexity and volatility, it's natural for them to seek support, direction, and meaning within groups or movements.

If anything, this trend will grow in the years ahead, Johansen maintains. "We're forecasting a permanently VUCA world," he says. "The problems are going to get worse before they get better, so movements will become increasingly important." Johansen is finding that more and more, "people want to engage on some level with the world around them, to feel as if they're making a difference. And they want to give their time, not just money."

That spirit is going strong among baby boomers, who are volunteering more and starting second careers geared toward social entrepreneurship. And it's also rising fast among younger people, who've grown up hyper-aware that the world has big problems and that somebody needs to step up and address them. The design activist John Bielenberg, who has launched a number of grassroots movements bringing together young designers and innovators to try to tackle social problems (Bielenberg is perhaps best known for an ongoing movement called Project M, which brings young designers into poverty-stricken areas to try to create change), says that he's seen a significant shift in the last few years. Young people have moved from being more career-oriented—"Before, it was all about getting a good job and your Saab convertible," Bielenberg says—to being more interested in the possibilities of applying their creative skills to larger issues and problems. "I don't think it's so much about, 'We're going to save the world,'" Bielenberg says. "It's more a matter of just wanting to use your talents for things you can feel passionate about."

In a number of the brand movements we've been involved with, we've seen firsthand that people seem to be looking for meaning and purpose, perhaps more than in the past. The True

North movement, discussed earlier, was rooted in the baby boomers' hunger to be part of something bigger and more meaningful than just their jobs. We've also found more recently that people of all ages are keenly aware that this is a time of profound challenges—and that those challenges are going to test our mettle as a society and as individuals. This became the driving idea behind a movement we launched recently on behalf of the Jim Beam spirits brand, under the banner of "Bold Choices" (it is featured in the next chapter). To sum it up, the idea is that this is no time for the timid; people know they're living in a world that's calling for them to take bold action. A lot of them seem to be ready and willing to do so, although they may need ideas, inspiration, and guidance in figuring out where to channel those energies and efforts. It may seem counterintuitive to think that brands can play a role in guiding people toward more purposeful choices and actions, but I believe they can—and I think we're already seeing some evidence of that.

THE RISE OF MARKETING 3.0

The Pepsi Refresh project is an outstanding example of what can happen when a brand—using its own marketing resources, aided and abetted by social media—successfully taps into this growing desire among people to do something constructive.

A couple of years ago, Pepsi took the $20 million it had earmarked for a handful of Super Bowl commercials (yes, believe it or not, that's how much it costs to produce a few ads and run them during the big game) and decided to do something dramatically different—it decided to launch a movement. The idea was to award that money to the people who came up with the best ideas for how to rebuild schools, fix up playgrounds, rejuvenate local communities, or do just about anything else that would have a positive "refreshing" effect on the world and on other people's lives. Project ideas were submitted and posted online, and the public could vote electronically on the best ideas. Grants ranging from $5,000 to $250,000 were then awarded to the top vote-getters.

Over the course of 2010, Pepsi awarded more than $20 million to about 1,000 projects. *Forbes* magazine cited it as one of the year's best social media campaigns, and here's why: not only did the Refresh Project contribute something meaningful to communities around the country, but it enabled Pepsi to connect with huge numbers of people in a positive way. The participants who were working on the projects—or just trying to get votes for their ideas—spread the word through social media, creating a swarm effect on behalf of Pepsi. So far, more than 80 million people have participated in the project by voting—in fact, as Pepsi's former marketing director Jill Beraud points out (see the interview with her in the sidebar), more people have voted in this movement than in any American election.

It's hard to imagine anything like Pepsi's Refresh Project being done even just a few years ago. For one thing, the role of social media in driving it forward was critical. But beyond that, this movement tapped into the growing restlessness among people who are hungry to get involved and to do something positive. It's also hard to imagine that a company the size of Pepsi would have been willing to take a step like this in the past, but it's a reflection of a shift in the corporate mindset that is just beginning to take hold.

MOVEMENT ## CAUSE MARKETING 2.0

EXEMPLAR   PEPSI REFRESH PROJECT

THE BIG IDEA   The Pepsi Refresh Project is a social media/philanthropic program that solicits ideas from consumers about improving their communities and then, via an interactive website, asks others to vote on each project to determine whether it should be funded. The submissions are divided into four categories: art & music, education, communities, and the Pepsi Challenge, which changes monthly. The grants are currently awarded in four increments: $5,000, $10,000, $25,000, and $50,000.

STARTED   PepsiCo started the Refresh Project in January 2010.

HOW IT SPREAD   In addition to the usual print and TV advertising, the Refresh Project was advertised on bottles and cans of Pepsi, with bottle cap promotions that offered up to 100 votes (a hybrid of loyalty program and crowdfunding). It also spread via word of mouth and social media, as competing projects would encourage their followers via Facebook and Twitter to go to the Refresh site and vote. The project itself has a robust website and its own Facebook page.

WHERE IT STANDS NOW   Pepsi says the Refresh Project has exceeded the company's goals for engaging consumers. More than 76 million votes have been cast, and more than $20 million has been invested in total: 78 parks and playgrounds improved, 123 schools improved, 21 foster homes and housing facilities repaired and/or built, and 163,000 lives improved directly. The program has been featured in thousands of local newspapers and television stories, mostly praising Pepsi for creating an innovative social media program. On the other hand, in its first year, the program did not produce positive sales results, which raised doubts about whether or how long Pepsi would stay behind it. It was revamped in 2011 to make it "more democratic" by changing its voting rules and policing the process to weed out voting fraud and level the playing field for smaller, grassroots projects.

QUOTE "The whole notion of allowing consumers to have a voice is really the wave of the future."—Jill Beraud, former chief marketing officer for PepsiCo Beverages America

WEBSITE Refresheverything.com

Procter & Gamble's Marc Pritchard has talked about a new approach to marketing—call it "Marketing 3.0"—that is just coming to the surface. "We're moving toward an inflection point," Pritchard said in a recent interview with *The Economic Times*. "We're shifting toward purpose-inspired brand building—a shift from marketing to serving." This is being done, he says, in response to consumers who have begun to ask questions about brands that they didn't ask in the past: "What does this brand really stand for? Does it share my values? Does it care about the things I care about?"

Here again, the rise of digital technology and social media plays a role in this change, because it has become so much easier for consumers to ask—and get answers to—these questions. The Internet has provided greater transparency, enabling the public to see what a company is doing and how it is behaving, and social media is enabling those same people to easily share what they've learned about a company. "The values revolution is being amplified by the digital revolution," according to Sebastian Buck, a co-leader of the agency GOOD/Corps (an offshoot of *Good* magazine). As Buck told the *New York Times*, "Customers can advocate both for and against companies, so companies have to be truly authentic. All brands are going to have to cross this threshold in terms of redefining themselves in this new culture."

A recent study by Edelman PR found that 87 percent of Americans believe that companies should be as concerned with societal interests as with business ones. Studies are also showing that people believe in this strongly enough that they will switch brands solely because of the values expressed and the causes supported by a brand.

The old, conventional way of responding to findings like these would be to say: "Fine, let's donate more money to charity." A company would pick a random good cause, throw money at it, and then run ads trumpeting these donations. Donations and sponsorships are wonderful and important, and I'd never want to discourage companies from doing that. But if that's all a company does, it can seem like a token gesture—just another form of PR. It tends to come across as passive and generic, rather than engaged and authentic.

I think the challenge for brands in this new environment is to try to find that sweet spot that connects with both people's growing interest in social issues and their desire to actually get involved themselves in making a difference. This is part of the beauty of movements—instead of the company taking it upon itself to support causes, now it can enable others to participate in worthwhile causes and endeavors. It's a more active, participatory, and authentic way for a company to get involved in the issues, interests, passions, and causes that really matter to people.

But how do you know which causes to get involved with? There are so many interesting initiatives and ideas out there, so many things that a brand could conceivably get behind and try to turn into a movement. Which ones are most likely to gain traction? And perhaps more important, which are most appropriate for your particular brand and business situation? We'll explore this in the next chapter, which is all about identifying "ideas on the rise."

AN INTERVIEW WITH PEPSI'S JILL BERAUD

As the former chief marketing officer for beverages, Americas, at PepsiCo, Jill Beraud helped spearhead a number of successful movements for the company, including the groundbreaking Refresh Project.

What's happening now that is making movements more important to people and to companies?

Technology is enabling people to rally around a movement and make things more global than ever before. I think there's always been an innate need and human desire to rally around an idea and create a movement, but it's been more isolated. The tools we have now have amplified the visibility of it, and enabled movements to take on a greater momentum.

Beyond just the technology aspect, it seems as if Pepsi's Refresh Project might be tapping into something that's in the air now—a desire to take on problems and get things done.

Yes, and that is exactly what we hoped would happen. This did not get created as a promotion idea; it came out of the DNA of the brand, that Pepsi has always been a catalyst for change. We wanted to empower people and their ideas—and help enable them to make things happen. So it wasn't about us coming up with ideas, it was about enabling consumers to come up with ideas that would move the world forward. And it was not about us choosing which ideas to fund, it was about other consumers choosing them.

Is organizing an effort like this harder to do than making ads?

It was an incredibly difficult, complex thing to pull off, because we needed to create the infrastructure for this—the platforms, the database, everything. It was a major commitment and a big investment. We not only put in a lot of money to fund the ideas, but also brought in ambassadors to mentor the people that we would actually fund—so it wasn't just about giving money, it was about helping people to nurture their ideas and make them successful.

It's been said that increasingly, brands are being judged not just on what they say in their ads, but on what they actually do. Do you agree?

Yes. We've talked about optimism a lot in our ads, but we wanted to walk the talk. And we wanted to actually practice what we were preaching—not just use words that would make people feel better, but actually make things happen that could help make the world a better place. It sounds very altruistic, I know. We also believed in this notion of social entrepreneurism and the democratization of creativity—which is something we learned from another brand, Mountain Dew.

Can you talk about what you did with that brand, in terms of building a movement?

"Dewmocracy" was one of the first mainstream consumer brand movements that was all about co-creating with consumers. We created new flavors, and they helped us pick the flavors, name the flavors, and pick the advertising and the media plan. We've done this a couple of years in a row, and it's been hugely successful for us. It creates a whole different level of engagement. And we found that consumers are so much more creative than anybody gives them credit for.

Going back to the Refresh Project, what have you learned from doing this—and what kind of results have you seen?

We learned a lot about what worked and what didn't. We had to make adjustments. For example, we learned that whoever could submit ideas first would get into the program, and that closed out a lot of people with good ideas, so we changed it to more of a lottery system. We also found that when we had $250,000 grants, we attracted big organizations. But we wanted to empower individuals, not large organizations. So now we're going to offer the same amount of money overall, but in smaller denominations ($50,000 is the highest level now).

In terms of results, we measured brand equity and participation, and here are a couple of fun facts: we've had more people vote in the program than have ever voted in any presidential election. And more people participated, in terms of trying to get grants for their ideas, than in any *American Idol* audition. We also have 20,000 visitors a month to our site, which is more than any Facebook account. So it has become a large media property. In terms of sales, we didn't want it to be too commercial, so we didn't tie it directly to sales. And as a result, our sales didn't necessarily lift because of it. But it was highly effective at changing our brand equity measurements—those went up double digits. In our second year, we'll tie a little more to sales by creating power votes—if you buy the product, you get extra voting power. But we still have to be careful about keeping this authentic.

Any advice to other marketers thinking of doing something like this?

The key is to be true to the brand and be authentic. You have to be transparent, and if you make any mistakes, you have to admit them, fix them, and move on. Give voice to your consumers, which is a very exciting thing to do, but it means giving up a little bit of control. Overall, I'd say marketers need to be courageous and not resist this. Embrace the change.

A MOVEMENT TO THE TRUE NORTH

It started when Jaya Kumar at Frito-Lay asked StrawberryFrog to help introduce a new kind of snack food, aimed at health-conscious baby boomers. In a product category that isn't known for healthiness or for innovation, this was an attempt to achieve both. So we felt that there might be a way to connect to some of the boomers' own desires to reach for a higher purpose.

As we did some cultural anthropology, one of the insights that surfaced had to do with boomers reaching their fifties and starting to think about their legacy. More and more, they were starting to ask themselves, "What is my life's one true passion?"

We made the term True North describe this calling—and then we set out to find the world's most inspiring True North stories. We reached out to the online community and invited people to share their own True North stories. We were amazed at the response; we'd come upon a movement that was actually quite strong, but that hadn't been articulated. This is when movements can become really powerful—when it's less about the story you're trying to tell everybody, and more about you giving people the tools and the platforms to tell their own stories.

We took some of the best stories and, working with the story-tellers, created a series of mini-documentary films that were put on the web, where they were quickly passed around and shared by others—which isn't surprising, because the stories were wonderful. They featured people who'd stepped away from their everyday routine lives to do things like starting a circus . . . creating an elephant sanctuary . . . opening a therapeutic horse-riding center. One story stood out above the rest: about a woman who opened the "Inspiration Café," a restaurant for homeless people. It became the subject of a short film that we hired the Academy Award winner Helen Hunt to direct. It ran during the Oscar telecast and was seen by millions. This gave an added boost to our True North movement, but the movement was already going strong by then and achieving very good business results. And no wonder, because this kind of passion—as exemplified by all these wonderful people who'd identified their purpose and were now living it every day—is not only inspiring, but downright infectious.

CHAPTER 5

Ideas on
the Rise

HOW TO FIND THEM
AND GET BEHIND THEM

There are some marketing assignments that are inherently exciting, but launching a new version of accounting software isn't one of them. So when Microsoft came to StrawberryFrog a few years back looking for ways to generate interest around the introduction of its new small business software, we almost had no choice but to look beyond the product for something to talk about.

We started, as we often do, by raising the question: what's going on in the culture right now that might somehow be relevant to this product? At the time, tech start-up ventures were popping up everywhere, it seemed. It was a great time to be a young entrepreneur with a big idea.

In many ways, technology had changed the game in terms of people's career paths. A cushy job within a big corporation was no longer the prize it had once seemed to be. Those jobs were scarce anyway because of downsizing, and the ones that did exist generally didn't stir the passions of people who were looking to seize opportunity in the new economy. It was bolder, more interesting, and maybe even more pragmatic to start your own business, rather than trying to fight the crowd for a low rung on the corporate ladder.

So we thought: what if we could somehow tap into this rising spirit of entrepreneurialism? Whenever you're trying to match up an idea like this with a business objective, you have to make sure it's a good fit. This one fit perfectly, in fact: most existing small businesses were already using the competitor, Quicken software, and getting them to switch was going to be tough. But if Microsoft could align with the millions of Americans who were starting their own businesses or working on that small business idea they'd always wanted to pursue, it could open up a new group of consumers for this product. Understanding this idea on the rise enabled us, working with a very creative client in Chris Capossela, to create a phenomenon that got people engaged, excited, and moving forward—in other words, a movement.

When you spark a movement, it's good to get things started with something that can get people's attention right from the beginning. For Microsoft, if you watch the videos on YouTube, you'll see thousands of parachutes falling over a small town in the middle of America, each one carrying a free copy of Microsoft's new software. We set the stakes high enough to let people know this was serious. The best business idea submitted would get Microsoft's backing, including $100,000 in start-up costs and free technical support.

What did we find? That a *lot* of people out there had business ideas they were eager to launch. Everybody's got his or her own version of, "I may work at a bank, but I've always wanted to start a rock 'n' roll car wash." But this contest was not designed to reward purely pie-in-the-sky ideas. On the website we set up, ideawins. com, participants submitted their ideas and business plans to a virtually live host, who grilled them on the practical details. We crossed the country in IDEAWINS vans, soliciting entries. From thousands of ideas, we narrowed it down to three finalists before selecting the winner—and by this time we'd generated tremendous viral activity on the Internet, as well as heavy news media coverage that began to follow the contest as if it were *American Idol*. In terms of business results, we blew the doors off. Microsoft had gone into the project hoping for half a million customer downloads of the new software. In the first month and a half, 1.5 million people downloaded it. But beyond that, an otherwise dull product came to be associated with a wave of entrepreneurial creativity and excitement.

Again, this was not the textbook way to introduce a new piece of business software. Just look in any of the tech publications and you'll find that everybody is focused on specs and features. We achieved differentiation by taking our heads out of the tech sand and thinking beyond the product, and even the category. Out there in the wider world is where you must look to try to find the big ideas that are changing, or are about to change, the culture we all share. We like to call these "ideas on the rise."

Finding these ideas can be the key to sparking or aligning with powerful movements. But it's not all that easy to do, because the ideas may not yet be obvious (they will be once they've fully risen, but you want to catch them while they're still rising). Moreover, you must find ideas that are right for the company, brand, and product involved. Capturing those ideas and figuring out what to do with them is a multifaceted process.

EAR-TO-THE-GROUND MARKETING

The process starts with gathering information and learning, and this must be done on two parallel tracks. The first one involves the consumer culture and the effort to answer the big question, "What's going on out there?" To hark back to the movement sociologist Neil Smelser, as discussed in the preceding chapters, it's all about *social strain* that creates some sense of dissatisfaction or restlessness. You want to locate the sources of that strain and friction.

One of the things we stress at StrawberryFrog is that people who are working on brands have to be aware of what's going on in the larger world—in culture, film, new media, politics, and books. It's important that you have your antenna up, looking for themes that seem to be just starting to bubble up, whether in the press or on Twitter or maybe on that smart little blog you've stumbled upon that nobody else knows about. These are the places where you'll find people talking about the things they're obsessed with, intrigued by, scared of, worried about, or fascinated by.

MOVEMENT EMPOWERING TEENS TO CHANGE THE WORLD

EXEMPLAR DO SOMETHING

THE BIG IDEA This is a movement to build character, citizenship, and confidence in young people via volunteerism. Do Something provides funding for young social entrepreneurs, using the power of online to get teens to take action on social change and causes offline. Currently, only 23 percent of young people (25 and under) actively volunteer. The hope is that by leveraging the web, television, mobile applications, and pop culture, the movement can create a generation of doers.

STARTED   The actor Andrew Shue and his friends founded Do Something in 1993.

HOW IT SPREAD   Interest in Do Something initially spread through early media attention brought about by the foundation's celebrity founder, Andrew Shue. Since August 2003, CEO Nancy Lublin has grown the foundation via online marketing and social media. It continues to partner with many youth-friendly celebrity endorsers (such as musicians Nelly, the Jonas Brothers, and Usher) and garner significant media coverage via their support. In 2008, it created the annual campaign Teens for Jeans with Aeropostale to raise awareness about the homeless.

WHERE IT STANDS NOW   Do Something is now considered one of the largest foundations in the United States that helps young people; 2 million young people are members of the foundation. The "Do Something Awards" air on VH1 and recognize people under the age of 25 who are making an outstanding difference in the world. The Do Something website has more than 23,000 pages of content, with half a million unique visitors each month.

QUOTE   "Young people have the time, the passion, the energy to be the change agents in our country. We need innovation, we need entrepreneurship to be fostered, and that's what Do Something's all about: inspiring and giving real assistance to young people who want to change the world." —Andrew Shue, cofounder

WEBSITE   Dosomething.org

At the time we were first dreaming up the True North movement, focused on boomers chasing their life passions, we were noticing stories popping up about "creating your second act in life," with people chucking it all to open a winery or join an overseas volunteer effort. Similarly, when we were working on Smart Car, we noticed the rise of a new generation of green awareness, though it wasn't as hard-core as the old. These were people who didn't necessarily want to turn their backs on commercialism; they wanted to find a smarter, savvier, more balanced approach to enjoying the things they really needed and loved, while getting rid of the "stuff" that was excessive and pointless. The playful sensibility of this new generation had been captured nicely in a popular web film, *The Story of Stuff*, and we wanted to pick up on the theme and give that audience a new spin on that movement.

And, as mentioned earlier, the Microsoft "Idea Wins" movement came out of what was happening in Silicon Valley and elsewhere. The strike-it-rich stories were all around, which led us to believe that people would be receptive to a movement that could help them take part in the start-up wave. (Subsequently, as the economy worsened, the need for entrepreneurial self-sufficiency became even more important as companies basically stopped hiring and laid off people in huge numbers. One of the victims of the 2008 economic crash, Eric Proulx, started a movement that dealt with how to turn the "lemon" of being laid off into "lemonade"; see sidebar interview).

If you look at some of the newer social movements that are popular right now, many of them can be traced to a social strain that may have existed for a while, but that has started to reach some kind of a tipping point—which then sparks the movement as a response. A great example of this is Dan Savage's remarkably successful "It Gets Better" movement. Savage, a columnist and author, started it all in the fall of 2010, in response to a series of recent incidents in which students had taken their own lives after being bullied at school. Savage went to YouTube and posted a video that he and his partner, Terry, had created that tried to rally others to send messages of support to young people, particularly those in the LGBT (lesbian, gay, bisexual, and transgender) community. The core message that Savage wanted to send became the movement's rallying cry: "It Gets Better."

Within a couple of months after Savage posted the first video, the movement had gone worldwide and inspired more than 10,000 user-created videos that had been viewed more than 35 million times. Messages were submitted by everyone from President Obama and Ellen DeGeneres to the staff of Google and the players on the Boston Red Sox. But according to Savage, the real driving force behind this now-thriving movement is the participation of everyday people. "The heart and soul of this project," Savage maintains, "are still the videos created by ordinary LGBT adults—people you haven't heard of—telling their stories, offering advice, sharing their coping strategies, and, in the comments threads, offering many LGBT kids something they've never had before: the ear of a sympathetic adult who understands exactly what they're going through."

MOVEMENT REDUCING TEENAGE SUICIDE

EXEMPLAR IT GETS BETTER

THE BIG IDEA Through YouTube videos posted by both famous and unknown people, the It Gets Better Project tells teenagers in the LGBT community that they are not alone and that their quality of life will get better.

STARTED In September 2010, after gay teenager Billy Lucas took his own life after being bullied by schoolmates, columnist and author Dan Savage created a YouTube video with his partner to relay the "It Gets Better" message.

HOW IT SPREAD The YouTube-based project quickly caught on, and within weeks it had garnered support from celebrities, organizations, sports teams, politicians, activists, and media personalities who uploaded their own inspiring messages. The success of the viral videos led to mainstream media coverage. A much-tweeted-about 90-second ad for the Chrome Browser by Google featured It Gets Better and aired repeatedly during prime time.

WHERE IT STANDS NOW The project is now organized on its own interactive website and includes more than 22,000 video entries and blog posts from people of all sexual orientations, including many celebrities. *It Gets Better*, a book of essays from the project, was released in March 2011.

QUOTE "We got an indication that this was going to be big in about 24 hours. The e-mails started pouring in to the account. And YouTube likes and e-mail forwarding, exploding on Twitter and Facebook. And after four days, when we reached 650 videos, it became clear we had touched a nerve." —Dan Savage

WEBSITE ItGetsBetter.org

In Savage's case, the idea on the rise—that there was a crisis developing with bullied teens and that people needed to step forth to offer support—came out of newspaper headlines, but sometimes you have to dig deeper to find these emerging issues. Fortunately, because of the social networking revolution, it's much easier today to actually connect with people to get a sense of what's on their minds as trends are just starting to come to the surface.

IS IT TIME TO TAKE A STAND ON SITTING?

For example, while using Twitter recently, we noticed a graphic that seemed to be spreading quickly. It showed the outline figure of a man sitting at a desk, with an ominous cloud hovering overhead and the words *sitting is killing you*. We did some digging and found that there were millions of Google searches on the subject of the hazards of sitting. We discovered some interesting stats: that sitting increases the risk of death up to 40 percent; that people with sitting jobs have twice the rate of cardiovascular disease as people with standing jobs; that we actually spend more time sitting at a desk than lying in bed. Then we found out that lots of people (including Beyoncé!) were promoting exercises for people who were stuck behind desks all day, and that "treadmill desks" were starting to catch on, too.

Taking in all of this, we started to think: who might want to partner with this particular "idea on the rise"? You could probably come up with a litany of products and services: a gym, a health food brand, and so on. But who better to align with a movement against the hazards of sitting than the very product that is involved in doing the damage—I'm thinking about a chair, of course. For a company such as HÅG, which creates chairs that are healthier and allow for more movement, it's a perfect fit. We've actually developed a brief for HÅG on how to create "a movement movement . . . that starts at your desk."

Just as an exercise, you might want to try this out yourself. Start looking for a theme that you're seeing repeatedly on Twitter or Facebook, or something that you're hearing in cocktail party chatter. Do some digging to see what's behind the trend in terms of supporting data. Then think about how a product or brand (not necessarily your brand, but any brand) might pick up on this trend and help generate some kind of response to it.

THE BRAND CULTURAL IDEAL

I mentioned earlier that there's a second parallel track that you must explore, in addition to investigating what's going on in the culture. Successful brand movements require not only that you understand cultural trends, but also that you understand the brand well enough to find the *right* cultural trends to seize upon. If you're in the marketing world in some capacity, you may figure you know brands pretty well—particularly the brand you're managing or working with. But we've found that there's a whole different level of understanding that has to be achieved, which we refer to as the "brand cultural ideal."

This is about finding and articulating the brand's ultimate purpose in the world. As shown in Figure 5-1, most brands tend to be focused on telling consumers about the outer *what* circle. This involves what they make or do—in other words, the product. The next circle in is *how* they do what they do, and the innermost circle is *why* they do what they do.

The reality is, people align with brands for mostly emotional reasons. They're not particularly moved by *what* we do or by *how*

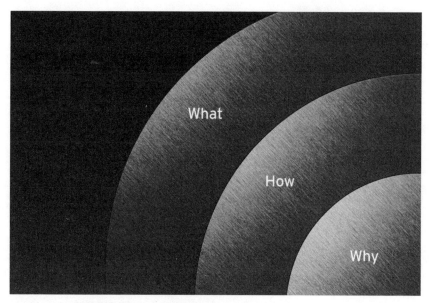

Figure 5-1 **Find the Truth in Your Brand**

we do it, but if we can get them to understand and appreciate *why* we do it, that tends to resonate. So the challenge is to let people into that inner circle—to communicate from the inside out.

But first, the company and its partners must, themselves, have a clear understanding of that higher purpose or truth that is at the core of the brand. Often, that purpose gets obscured over time; maybe it was never clearly defined or articulated at the start. In any case, if a brand is going to align with purposeful movements, it must first clarify its own purpose.

At times, we've found ourselves trying to help clients dig out this deeper truth by asking them to consider fundamental questions: In what way does your company actually affect people's lives? Why did the company start doing this in the first place? What are the values that this brand lives by? What is the brand trying to achieve, ultimately? What does the company believe in? What does the brand really stand for?

Whether they admit it or not, people are looking for this sense of purpose in a brand (and, as we noted in the previous chapter's discussion of the rise of "Marketing 3.0" or purpose-driven marketing, they seem to be looking for it more than ever these days). From the company's standpoint, uncovering this purpose can be a matter of digging into the founders' history or the heritage of a brand. Alternatively, it may be a matter of taking the basic benefit that a product provides and thinking about it more expansively.

Just as a hypothetical, suppose you had a certain liquid product that cleans the house (and whose mascot may or may not be a certain iconic bald-headed guy). Beginning with this rather unexciting core benefit, cleaning up the house, here's how you might extrapolate from it in terms of thinking about a movement. First, consider what's happening in society at the moment, such as:

- Because of the economy, people can't afford to hire cleaners anymore.

- One of the ways relationships between parents and kids are changing is that they're not doing family chores together the way they once did.

- Do-it-yourself (DIY) home improvement is on the rise.

Considering these trends, you might, for instance, explore a movement idea that promotes families working together to increase cleanliness in the home while saving money—a kind of family DIY cleaning movement. Would it catch on? You'd have to do some deeper investigation of current cultural attitudes to see if that particular idea resonates. But my point is this: somewhere, even in the most mundane products, there are possibilities that can lead to a more meaningful sense of purpose.

WHAT ARE YOU AGAINST?

One way to clarify what it is you stand for is to start by figuring out what you're *against*. As we saw in Chapter 2, Volkswagen took on big cars, and Apple took on Big Brother (aka IBM). I mentioned in that chapter that our own Smart Car movement took on overconsumption by declaring that we were "Against Dumb." But that's just one of many examples in which StrawberryFrog figured out who or what the "brand nemesis" was before launching a movement. In fact, almost every one of our movements is against something. We developed a global movement for Cap Gemini Ernst and Young, where we created a volatile character called "The Economy"—and then challenged our audience to "Defy the Economy" by becoming adaptive. As for the Microsoft "Idea Wins" campaign that started this chapter it was not just a statement *for* entrepreneurial risk–taking; it was also *against* following the typical career path by climbing the corporate ladder.

It is critical that a movement have something to move against. The late author Eric Hoffer, who wrote extensively about social movements, once said: "Mass movements can rise and spread without belief in God—but never without belief in a devil." Having a nemesis to rail against really stirs people up and helps them to bond together. Just look at the Tea Party; as political movement guru Mark McKinnon points out in the accompanying interview (see sidebar interview), it's a movement born out of opposition and fueled by deep anger at perceived enemies. All of this has helped the movement to grow rapidly, although, as McKinnon notes, if the Tea Partiers can't get past being mad all the time, the movement may not mature and endure.

MOVEMENT GRASSROOTS POLITICAL REFORM

EXEMPLAR   NO LABELS

THE BIG IDEA   No Labels is a nonpartisan advocacy organization designed to bring together leading thinkers from the left, the right, and all points in between. The multipartisan group works together to create a better method of coming up with solutions and to ensure equal news coverage of *all* political parties. A second goal is to facilitate the aggregation and collection of citizens' views and opinions to be heard as one voice via social media and online organizing technology.

STARTED   Nancy Jacobson, Mark McKinnon, John Avlon, Kiki McLean, and more than a dozen others founded No Labels in December 2010.

HOW IT SPREAD   No Labels has heavyweight politicians and celebrities behind it. It hosted a series of "Road Shows" in which senior leaders traveled to specific cities to have discussions about the No Labels movement with local citizens. Also, it hosted well-publicized "State of the Unity" gatherings the night of the 2011 State of the Union address. No Labels issues press releases naming politicians for their good or bad actions on behalf of bipartisanship. Its website and social media also foster involvement, with a Twitter hashtag #NoLabels and asking people to sign an online No Labels

Declaration. In offline life, people are recruited to serve as Citizen Leaders and asked for donations.

WHERE IT STANDS NOW   No Labels continues to form alliances with other citizens' movements, such as Howard Schultz's Upward Spiral. There are more than 80,000 Citizen Leaders for No Labels. In June 2012 there will be a No Labels National Convention in Philadelphia.

QUOTE   "Since its beginning, No Labels has been out in front on the need for 'everyone at the table, everything on the table' to solve our country's financial challenges. Tens of thousands of our members have contacted Congress, urging them to change the tone of these contentious debates and find a way to work together to address this issue." —Mark McKinnon, cofounder

WEBSITE   Nolabels.org/front

For some reason, it can be easier to figure out what you're against than to figure out what you're for—maybe because what you are pursuing is often elusive, whereas the thing you're against is usually standing directly in the way. Keep in mind, however, that it's important to think about pursuits and obstacles not in terms of your own interests, but of your customers'. What is it that *they* desire (that you can help provide), and what is standing in the way of that? Identifying that obstacle will help you identify your brand nemesis. It may be that you're championing some kind of new approach or new way of doing things; if so, you can take a stand against the old, entrenched ways or status quo attitudes. Or, conversely, you might be defending tradition by taking on trendy new attitudes and behaviors. Either way, there's no shortage of things worth taking a stand against.

(One caveat: don't simply take a stand against your competition. You may hate your competitor's guts, but nobody else cares; the outside world is looking for you to take on something more meaningful and interesting. Now if your competitor can be used to represent something larger and more meaningful to people—à la IBM and "Big Brother"—then you may be on to something.)

It certainly helps when the thing you're taking a stand against is big and malevolent. One of the most effective public service advertising movements in recent years was the "Truth" teen antismoking campaign, overseen by the American Legacy Foundation, which did a great job of rallying teenagers against smoking. Historically, it's been difficult to get teens to care about the fact that smoking can harm them later in life—that's just too far removed from their present-day concerns, so there's no "strain" or dissatisfaction to light that initial spark. But in this case, what resonated with teens was the idea that a nemesis was trying to manipulate and harm them. The "Truth" campaign showed the various ways in which Big Tobacco companies have lied, obfuscated, targeted youth, contributed to disease and death, and gotten rich in the process. The righteous anger stoked by that movement got teenagers engaged and involved in the cause, and led to significant declines in teen smoking.

But you don't necessarily need an enemy as ideal as Big Tobacco; it could be something as harmless as bland food. Our client Sabra, which makes hummus, faced a challenge in that some Americans viewed it warily as "foreign" food. We saw an interesting friction at work here. Today, more and more Americans are looking to expand their cultural horizons and adopt a larger worldview. And yet their eating habits and food choices often lag behind. We tend to play it safe and go for the familiar with food choices. So the "nemesis" here was the predictable and unadventurous culinary habits of Americans, which are at odds with the rise of a more global, multiethnic, multicultural society. To sharpen it a bit more, you could say that the villain here is xenophobia, encompassing everything from harsh anti-immigrant rhetoric to chants of "USA first!" (but let's not get too political; it's only hummus we're talking about).

In any case, we used old and new media to push out this idea, and we did unconventional things like set up a multicity chefs' tour and house parties around the country, where people could actually set aside the Cheez Whiz and give hummus a try. We also wanted to give folks a way to take action on this "adventurous eating" theme, so we created the "Sabra Taste Intervention"—kind of a playful twist on the idea of using interventions to help people with hoarding and other problems. In this case, if you knew someone who had fallen into a "food rut," you could use social media to nominate that person for a culinary makeover. The winner of the contest was a Philadelphia fireman, who was promptly whisked away to Turkey for a week of amazing eating experiences—which were then filmed and turned into a web series to help fuel the next stage of the movement.

THE LITMUS TEST: IS IT CREDIBLE?

The big question is, if you get behind a larger cultural idea or align with some kind of movement, will people accept your brand in that role? Will it be seen as credible? A lot of this depends on whether your behavior with regard to the movement is consistent with your behavior the rest of the time. When a company like Kentucky Fried Chicken tries to align itself with a movement like fighting breast cancer, it can be a tough sell with the public. As the *Washington Post* and others noted (for complete clarity, I'm not the one saying this, the *Post* is!), KFC produces food that could conceivably be seen as contributing to health problems. So there's a disconnect there—or, perhaps, the sense that the company might be supporting this cause in order to try to make amends. Within any kind of movement, people are very sensitive to outsiders who may be trying to co-opt their passion and energies and use them for the wrong reasons. Even a somewhat playful movement like "taste intervention" could be undermined if, say, the company supporting it made unhealthy food: "You're trying to get me to encourage my friends and family to experiment with something that's bad for them?" It just doesn't work.

It's also important that there be some kind of logical connection between what the brand stands for and what the movement is about. If there isn't it can look as if you just picked a random issue or movement that seemed popular, and jumped on board. If there isn't some kind of synergy between the brand and the movement, then even if the movement is a success, it won't help the brand.

If we look at a movement like the Pepsi Refresh Project, there's a connection there that has to do with what that brand has stood for throughout its history. Going back to when Pepsi introduced the idea of the "Pepsi Generation," this brand has always been associated with youth, change, and rebirth—which is a big part of the spirit of the Refresh movement.

MAKING A BOLD CHOICE

As I mentioned earlier, sometimes the core values of a brand—the values that might align with those of a movement—can be found in the company's history. Recently, we were working with Jim Beam, one of American's most iconic brands, on revitalizing the brand. The outcome was the "Bold Choice" movement, which is championing the idea that we all need to be willing to take on more demanding challenges, especially in today's world. This felt like an idea that was definitely rising up in the culture.

But as we dug into the brand's history, we began to see that "Bold Choice" actually reflected not just the product, but also the attitude that helped this company survive and move forward in some tough times. Kevin George, who heads up the Beam brand (and who, as you may recall from Chapter 2, was also involved in the Dove "Real Beauty" movement), explains that the idea of "Bold Choice" was really "born out of the DNA of this brand."

"With any movement, I think you have to figure out how it's linked intrinsically to what the brand stands for," George says. "When we hit upon the idea of bold choices and the people who make those choices—and celebrating that—we felt this was an interesting possibility. So we went back and revisited every element of the brand: what it stood for in the consumer's mind, what we wanted it to be, the heritage of it. We were able to identify a few things around 'bold,' one being the flavor of the product—and the idea that consumers are looking for that, in a more 'flavorful world.' But more important, as we considered what the brand and the family are about, we discovered that this is a family that made some interesting and bold choices to get where it is today.

Whether it was going to Kentucky to make bourbon, or starting up a distillery again after Prohibition—and doing it within 120 days after all that time—those kinds of choices fit with this idea."

As is often the case, the idea was tested out initially with some consumers to see how they'd react. "What we heard from consumers is, 'I don't want to follow the crowd; I want to be seen as the kind of guy who thinks for himself and chooses things that are a little more distinctive,'" George says. "So for us, it all came together around this idea 'Bold Choices'—this notion that the choices you make in life end up dictating the life you lead. And that all choices lead you somewhere, but bold choices take you where you're supposed to be."

George says that through embracing this idea, there was a change in how the brand felt about itself and its mission. (We'll explore this more in the next chapter—that a movement can and should take hold *within* the culture of a company before it goes to the outside world, and that, ideally, the company's employees should be the first ones to rally around and be changed by that idea.) "This lifted up the brand to stand for something bigger—not only as a brand, but as a company," he says.

The task now for the Jim Beam brand (and for us, as its partner) is to build on this idea and create multiple expressions of it—multiple platforms where people can engage with this philosophy— and to find as many ways as possible to encourage people to start making bold choices in their own lives and in the world around them. "As it evolves, we'll have stories and discussion around this idea. We may grab onto current events and celebrate bold choices there, too—from our political leaders doing the right thing to the coach who makes a tough call on fourth down," George says. "We want to celebrate that, but we also will find ways to help the people in this movement make their own bold choices. I think we're at a time now where the recession is lifting a bit, and there's an opportunity for people to feel more comfortable stepping up and taking on challenges—maybe trying to do things that are riskier, that they wouldn't have pursued a couple of years ago." George freely acknowledges that "all of this can seem pretty high-minded, for a bourbon brand to be talking about these big life decisions. But at the same time, we believe in this whole idea of elevating brands to have a positive impact on culture." (A testament to Kevin George's vision is the fact that *Time* magazine named "Bold Choices" among the Top 10 best advertising of 2011.)

WRITING A MANIFESTO

If you think you've got a good fit between a movement idea and the brand, but you're still not absolutely sure, one early way to test your comfort level and the depth of your belief in the concept is to write a manifesto. It's a chance to summarize, and crystallize, your views on this subject, and a chance to test out your movement "voice" and see if it rings true.

The manifesto could be just for you and your company; then again, you might end up going public with it as the movement launches. For Smart Car, the manifesto we wrote "against dumb" became our rallying cry to the public:

Why do so many smart people do dumb things?

We buy stuff we don't need, left and right—that's dumb.

We buy things without the least concern for the planet—that's even dumber.

We buy things from the "Skystore catalog"—Dumbest. Move. Ever.

Dumb is Venti when tall is plenty.

Dumb requires multiple remotes.

Dumb is two-for-one, when all you are is one.

Dumb is eating anything bigger than your head.

Dumb thinks 12 mpg is A-OK.

When it comes to consuming things, America's got a fever of a hundred and dumb.

And there's only one prescription—to get smart about our stuff.

By having just the right stuff. Not all of it.

By buying what we need and borrowing what we can.

So long, battery-operated paper towel dispenser.

We don't need you anymore. Come to think of it, we never did.

Let's put an end to mindless consumption.

Let's take the junk out of our collective trunk.

That's the whole idea behind Smart—we're against dumb.

Come join us.

A manifesto gets everyone on the same page. It forces clarity and focus.

If you can't write a manifesto—if you can't articulate a potential movement in strong, unequivocal, and hopefully inspiring language—then you may have a problem before you even begin.

WHAT ARE YOUR OBJECTIVES?

The final thing to think about as you decide whether to embrace the big idea and try to start a movement behind it involves asking yourself what you really want to get out of all this. Yes, of course, you want to increase sales and brand loyalty and gain market share—all of those reasonable business objectives. But in terms of the movement itself, what do you want people to actually *do*? Contribute ideas? Hold rallies? Adopt dogs? Keep in mind that a movement is about people taking action together to change something—so think about what the action should be, what the change is likely to be, and what all of this means, ultimately, to you and your brand.

And think about what your role will be in all this. What assets can you apply or offer toward this objective? How involved do you want to be in this collective endeavor?

MOVEMENT ELIMINATING DISTRACTED DRIVING

EXEMPLAR   NO PHONE ZONE WHILE DRIVING PLEDGE

THE BIG IDEA   Oprah Winfrey harnessed her celebrity power and her vast audience to launch a campaign to encourage drivers not to use handheld devices for phone calls, to pull over if they have to use their cellphone, and not to text while driving.

STARTED   Oprah Winfrey started the campaign in January 2009.

HOW IT SPREAD   Oprah talked up the movement extensively on her show, highlighting the stories of teens and adults who had lost their lives by using their cellphones while driving. On the highly trafficked Oprah website, there are numerous background articles and online calls to action, asking people to pledge not to text or talk on the phone while driving.

WHERE IT STANDS NOW   Two years after the campaign started, more than 400,000 Americans had pledged to stop using their cellphones while driving. A "No Phone Zone" web page is still up on Oprah's site (supported by big-name advertisers), and supporters can subscribe to a topical newsletter and participate in forums.

QUOTE   "If you think you can call, text, and drive at the same time, you cannot. That message you can't wait to send could kill. Distracted driving is an epidemic that is sweeping through our country, claiming lives and destroying families." —Oprah

WEBSITE   Oprah.com/packages/no-phone-zone.html

It's a good idea to try, to the extent this is possible, to envision the results up front. If you think of it in terms of input, output, and outcome, everything you do on your end to spark the movement (e.g., sharing content, giving people platforms, offering incentives) is input; the reaction of the community (conversations, co-created content, advocacy) is output. But what's going to matter most to your business in the end is outcome: what do you really hope these communities will do, and how will that build the business?

We'll explore outcomes more in the pages ahead, but one reason it's important to consider all of this up front is that movements can take off more quickly than you might expect. As Jim Beam's Kevin George attests, "This all moves very fast now. In the past, you'd create a movement by essentially trying to tell one person to tell another and another, and so on," and it could take decades for a movement to build. But now, with new movements operating at Internet speed, you can be part of something large overnight.

George is seeing that with his brands; Pepsi saw it happen even faster with the Refresh Project, where suddenly the company is involved in something new, large, and complex. So a question for any brand to consider is, do you want to take on the work that comes with having a deeper, more engaged, more complex relationship with consumers?

If the answer is yes, you're ready to launch—and that's what we'll cover in the next chapter.

TURNING A LEMON INTO "LEMONADE"—ERIK PROULX

After being laid off from his job in advertising, Erik Proulx decided to do something about it. He made a film profiling 16 advertising professionals who'd lost their jobs—and ended up finding their calling. The film, made entirely with money raised by donations, quickly gained word-of-mouth momentum within the creative communities and beyond, and "Lemonade" became a rallying cry of hope and personal reinvention in the midst of a painful recession. Its success has led Erik to launch a new movement called "Lemonade Detroit," this time highlighting the people who are working to reinvent and rebuild the Motor City.

How did this all get started?

"Lemonade" happened after I got laid off in the fall of 2008. I created a blog, "Please Feed the Animals," with the message to other ad people that it wasn't the end of the world to lose their jobs and that it actually could mean they could be placed in a better situation. Reinvention of my life and giving hope to the others in my situation spun the idea for "Lemonade." I decided I had to make the film. I had never made a film before, so it wasn't like I had a road map. But when you have a good idea and it is important to other people, they become interested. Really talented people wanted to get involved after hearing about the film. One phenomenal thing was everyone who discovered it was driven through social media: Twitter, Facebook, blogs. It literally would not have been possible without Twitter. Virgin America sponsored the flights, and it came about through a blog and Twitter. We blogged to Virgin asking for sponsorship, and it got retweeted and they got bombarded through that avenue. It was powerful.

What helps a movement draw attention?

The biggest thing my project had going for it was that there was and is a general global dissatisfaction with life as it is. Everyone wants to live the results of bold decisions and wants to reinvent. I don't think anybody really wants to just work at a job anymore . . . no one wants to punch in and out. Meanwhile, vast majorities of companies just look at their employees as a numbers game. You are considered an expense, and when times are bad, they get rid of the expense. If that's the case, we have to find a way to make a living that is meaningful. That is becoming embedded and engrained in everyone's subconscious: how can I do what I like now and still support myself?

What are the most important factors that help spark a movement, and what role can brands play?

Movements are created by dissatisfied people. Companies that want to be part of that need to provide a solution. Companies can be part of the movement and usher movement, but uprisings happen by the people. As long as there is a natural fit or an outlet or something that can answer that dissatisfaction, that movement can flourish and can be a genuine, nonmanufactured phenomenon.

Is it hard work? Is it satisfying?

There is definitely a lot of nail biting just because I threw myself into it. My wife does not work; we have two kids. . . . I would just film and work on it most days and then remotely freelance; 10 or 11 p.m. would be the beginning time for me to start my freelance work. It was blind faith, and I kept saying, "It has to work. It's going to work. It's the right thing to do," and ultimately it worked out.

POLITICAL MOVEMENT GURU
MARK McKINNON

Mark McKinnon has guided winning presidential campaigns and has been involved in successful causes such as Nike/Lance Armstrong's "LIVESTRONG" movement for cancer survivors. After being involved in trench warfare on both sides of the political divide, he's now forming a movement to try to find common ground between Democrats and Republicans.

You've started movements on behalf of candidates, brands, and now a bipartisan political movement, "No Labels." What have you learned about the keys to starting a movement?

I think the common element of all movements is that you don't start them; they start themselves. And all we do as marketers is try to tap into something—a spark that already exists—and figure out ways to channel it. The key is to do some pattern recognition, get out in front of whatever is happening, and try to find ways to harness it. And that's absolutely the case with "No Labels." I've been in politics for years, and successful politics is always about trying to anticipate where the market's going. Successful politicians always figure out where the next movement is heading.

The Tea Party is a great example of a movement that caught fire on its own and became a significant political movement. The No Labels effort is in some ways not necessarily a response to that, but a reaction to what's been happening on both sides. For lots of reasons, the political system in recent years has changed into one that has become hyperpartisan—it's dominated by the extremes on the left and right, and they don't really represent the majority. But because of the media tools available to them today, they've figured out ways to dominate the conversation and have an inordinate impact on the process. This has had a lot of implications and consequences—one being that they are really controlling political behavior in our campaigns and politics. Again, this doesn't really represent where the majority of Americans are. So from my work and travels, I see a huge gap there. People are saying to me, "Listen, the Tea Party doesn't represent me, MoveOn doesn't represent me—so who represents our voice any more, the vast middle of America?"

So it's a movement responding to movements on both sides—by creating one in the middle. How are you trying to build it?

We're using the technology and tools available to us to try to organize. In our first six months, we got about 80,000 members. We have a lot of different objectives, one being to make sure people know who we are—we've accomplished that, particularly with the media and political elites. I wanted to make sure we'd be seen as a credible source and voice in the media, and we've done that. We're being called to referee the debate on the media, which is what we wanted to do. Now we're in the process of organizing all over the country; we're going to have leaders in all the 435 congressional districts, plus chapters all over the country, college chapters at 100 universities, meet-ups all over the country.

How big a role are technology and social media playing in the rise of movements?

They're such easy connectors and a glue to bring together like-minded people. It's hard to imagine being able to leverage movements the way we can today without those tools.

People can organize really easily around specific interests. If you're a gun owner and pro-choice and believe in constitutional limits, you can organize around those ideas, or one of those ideas. Movements are happening now because we have the ability to organize around an idea because of all these new tools. There's always been, in some form or fashion, a frustration with the system—now there's a way to take on the system.

What made the Tea Party work as a movement?

It was successful because it was bottom-up. And part of the reason it grew so quickly is that it became a broad net for anger at the government. Period. Just as Obama was hope, the Tea Party was anger—if you were angry, this was the place to cast your lot. Then there was a period where it was unclear and chaotic and messy. And then somewhere along the line it got more clear about its message, and it became very constitutionally focused—it's really developed a focus on protecting the fundamentals of the Constitution, and in a way that made the brand clearer. But it's likely to suffer some decline just because of the realities—it got a bunch of people elected to Congress who are not going to be able to make the changes the Tea Party people want. With a movement like this—or, on the other side, Obama's movement—people become very excited, and everyone imposes his or her own ideas about what it represents. And if it doesn't represent everything people thought, or if the change doesn't happen as quickly as they hoped, the movement can quickly lose some of that enthusiasm.

CHAPTER 6

Lighting the Spark

You've identified and crystallized an idea that's on the rise in the culture. You're ready to turn it into a full-fledged movement. Where do you begin?

Surprising as it may seem, the best place to start building a business-driven consumer movement is within the company itself. This is an important part of what distinguishes movement marketing from more traditional marketing and advertising. Any company can say just about anything in an ad; the company doesn't necessarily have to live by those words or change its behavior to be in alignment with those words (yes, some companies do actually live up to their ad slogans, and that's great—but many do not). But a company can't really lead a successful consumer movement unless the beliefs, attitudes, and behaviors associated with that movement are well grounded within the company.

And that may require changing the culture within the company so that it matches up better with the ideals of the movement. This can be a significant undertaking, and one that we'll explore in this chapter. We'll also consider the ways in which a company can figure out, at the outset, how to better connect with a core community of "true believers," how to align a brand's assets and strengths with people's needs, and how to make sure that the various pieces are in place prior to the actual rollout of the movement. To a great extent, what you do before the first public shot is fired can have a major impact on whether the movement will prosper or fizzle.

Let's start with culture, and with a legitimate question: why might a company want to consider changing its own internal culture just because it is launching some type of external marketing movement? After all, companies don't typically put themselves through a cultural or philosophical overhaul every time they launch a new marketing campaign. Why should a brand movement be any different?

The main reason is this: if you identify the right movement to get behind, it's likely to be one that touches on, and brings to the surface, some of your core values as a company. And as this is unfolding, what you may discover is that those core values need to be clarified, articulated, strengthened, and acted upon—not just in an outward-facing campaign, but also internally. In other words, it may be necessary for your company to reaffirm and even to relearn what it stands for—and to take a stand *inside* the company before it takes a stand in the outside world.

A great example is Apple Computer. I know people get tired of hearing business writers sing the praises of Apple when it comes to everything from product design to packaging to marketing. But a lesser-known part of the story is that Apple built its movements (and note the use of the plural, because Apple has really launched a series of movements through the years) by starting from within, building a company culture that could drive and support the movement once it went public. When Steve Jobs returned to the company in the late 1990s, before launching the brand's famous "Think Different" campaign, he knew that his first job was to plant a flag within Apple with a rallying cry that could inspire his product developers and everyone else. Before the outside world ever saw "Think Different" ads, those two words were appearing on banners and T-shirts at the company's headquarters, ensuring that everyone at the company lived and breathed this philosophy. By the time "Think Different" became a public campaign—and a movement that rallied creative people everywhere around this idea—it was already an established mantra within Apple.

Lee Clow, the veteran creative chief at TBWA Worldwide and Jobs's longtime collaborator on Apple marketing campaigns, says: "The biggest compliment I ever got from Steve was when he told me 'Think Different' was more important to the company than it was to the consumer. Because that mantra told people inside the company, 'We are going to get back to the values and the soul of the Apple brand.' Steve was inviting everybody in that company to rethink everything. At the time, he didn't have any new product yet, and Apple was almost out of business. But to him, the first mission was to get everybody singing off the same song sheet again."

THE IMPORTANCE OF THE EARLY AMBASSADORS

One of the reasons why this kind of cultural alignment is so important is that a company's employees are, in a sense, the early ambassadors of any brand movement. They're the ones who will first begin to carry the message to the outside world—or fail to do so. They're the ones who will, through their workaday behaviors and actions, live up to the movement's ideals—or not live up to them.

And if they're true believers in that message and those ideals, their passion can be powerful and contagious. When you can connect a disparate, multidisciplinary community of individuals around a higher purpose, you can overcome tremendous obstacles. You can also change a company in profound ways that extend to structure, philosophy, behavior, corporate policy and procedure, and everything else.

On the other hand, it's not easy building a movement within a company—it can be a large and ambitious exercise in change management. It may take months or even years (or, to look at it another way, it never ends; transforming a corporate culture tends to be an ongoing process). But it's central to succeeding in movement marketing. Moreover, I'd argue that it is central to succeeding in business today.

Putting aside all discussion of movements for a moment, this connects to a larger conversation that's taking place across the business landscape these days, one regarding the increasing need for companies to develop strong internal cultures that foster certain values, and that focus not just on what a company makes or does, but also on *how* it acts and behaves.

It's an idea that is embodied in companies like Zappos, whose dedication to creating a great internal culture has become near-legendary. It's articulated in the writing of business gurus like Dov Seidman, whose "How" philosophy connects ethical corporate culture and behavior to strong performance. What Zappos,

Seidman, and many others have begun to recognize is that we're now operating in a world that increasingly expects and demands more from business. This is particularly true if you're leading some type of brand movement, but it's also true for business in general. In a time of greater transparency and higher consumer expectations, companies today are being watched and judged more closely in terms of how they behave.

This makes it imperative that businesses build internal cultures that can stand up to scrutiny and live up to our highest values. How do you do it? StrawberryFrog has had a crash course in this over the past couple of years, as we've endeavored to help several clients prepare to embark on an external movement by first launching an internal movement. A great case in point—and a particularly challenging one, if only in terms of the sheer size and scale involved—involves the Mahindra Group.

A CORPORATE CULTURE ON THE "RISE"

Mahindra is an India-based family of companies producing everything from aerospace technology to automobiles to software, and employing upwards of a million people worldwide. The company felt it needed to find a core purpose that could carry it into the future and unite a diverse group of people working in a range of industries. As we worked with it to try to crystallize that idea, there seemed to be a common thread between what Mahindra was now trying to do as a company—break new ground and pursue a larger purpose—and what many people around the world were also hungry to do on an individual basis, in response to the challenges facing everyone today. Mahindra's research found that a growing number of people wanted to shape their own destiny, solve problems in new ways, and contribute to the world around them. To put it more succinctly, they wanted to "rise" to the challenges of today.

The opportunity for Mahindra was to figure out how to encourage and enable people to rise to those challenges—this was the basic movement idea, and it was summed up in the line: "We will challenge conventional thinking and innovatively use all our resources to drive positive change in the lives of our stakeholders and communities across the world—to enable them to rise." It was an idea that in many ways was a good fit with the company's heritage: via its own ingenuity and ambition, Mahindra had risen from modest beginnings in India to become a global force. But that history notwithstanding, the company knew that it needed to rekindle some of that fire in its own workforce today before it took the message and the movement to the outside world.

The "Rise" theme offered the potential of being highly motivating internally because it was rooted in the idea of accepting no limits and using ingenuity to drive positive change. For Mahindra as an organization, "Rise" means "achieving world-class standards in everything we do, setting new benchmarks of excellence, and conquering tough global markets," noted Anand Mahindra, the managing director of Mahindra Group. But it also worked on an individual level: for employees working within a very large organization whose history involves traditional industries, "Rise" offered permission to innovate and set new goals—a potential break from ingrained practices and old ways of doing business. If you contrast that kind of message with something that a more traditional, product-focused or service-focused ad campaign might be likely to say ("Built to last" or "Close to the customer," for example), it offers a lot more for people within the company to latch onto, in terms of providing motivation and inspiration.

Introducing an inspiring new philosophy to the company culture is only a first step, of course; the words are just words unless there is something concrete to back them up. Our process of working with Mahindra on cultural transformation took more than a year. It started with an internal discovery process that involved talking to senior managers across the company about how they work, their goals and values, and their own perceptions of the company. One of the main objectives here was to clarify and better articulate the higher purpose of the brand. From the standpoint of a company and its employees, you must get to the essence of *why* you do what you do (as opposed to *what* you do or technically *how* you do it).

You're also looking to see if there is a gap between the company's ideals and its actual behavior. To the extent that such a gap exists, it's best if the people inside the company come to this realization on their own. One approach StrawberryFrog uses is to hold "mirror workshops" designed to reflect to a company the present realities of the company's culture and behavior—which will usually provide a pretty good idea of areas that may need to be addressed or changed.

There are any number of tools that can help build a strong corporate culture around a movement idea. Training programs are helpful, although we find they work best when they're interactive—not one-way indoctrination, but participatory discussion and brainstorming throughout various levels of the company. The idea is to get everyone directly involved in embracing the new idea and in finding ways to incorporate it into their work lives. So in the case of "Rise," the people at the company were challenged to think about how this idea might be applied or adapted to their own situations.

HAVE YOU ANYTHING TO DECLARE?

It helps if the idea you're trying to rally people around is clearly and forcefully articulated. We like to use the term *declare*: You must state this movement idea in a way that sounds like a declaration of something that has meaning and importance. Corporate mission statements, unfortunately, are often fuzzy, generic, and largely uninspiring to the troops. A movement declaration has to be more powerful than that, because it really does have to *move* people toward action.

While a declaration can be as concise as one sentence—see Mahindra's "We will challenge conventional thinking" line, as quoted previously—it can also be expanded into a larger statement that takes the form of a manifesto that may be a page or two in length. We talked briefly about manifestos in the previous chapter, in terms of how it can be useful to articulate and write down some movement principles to help you determine whether a particular "idea on the rise" is a good fit for your brand or your company. But a manifesto can also be a valuable tool as you begin to launch a movement within your company, and later, as you take that movement to the outside world. In fact, it can be useful throughout the life of a movement because it serves as a compass—if you start to lose sight of what the movement is about or if it begins to go off the rails in some way, the manifesto is there to remind everyone of the defining principles. If you do a manifesto for your brand movement (and I recommend that you do so), approach the writing of it as a serious challenge. To be effective, a manifesto has to be well thought out and strong worded. It should be passionate, but it also must be authentic. A manifesto that doesn't ring true to people—one that sounds as phony or as empty as a typical corporate mission statement—can do more harm than good if it suggests to employees that this whole movement thing is just the latest bit of corporate spin.

In some cases, and particularly if you're trying to institute fairly radical changes in the company culture, you may need to expand the manifesto into a small brand book—an internal bible that lays out the new belief system. We've done that with a number of our clients. A book provides room to explain and even illustrate ideas associated with the movement. It also offers an opportunity to let people know about ways the company may be changing to live up to the movement's ideal, including policy changes, operational changes, and so on.

And it may, indeed, be necessary to change company policies and procedures when you're launching a movement within a corporate culture. Words in manifestos are great, but actions, of course, speak louder. One of the things we do is brainstorm with companies on bold actions they could institute within the company as a way of signaling to everyone who works there, "It's a new day." (Google did something like this when it implemented "20 percent time" at the company, meaning that employees could devote 20 percent of their time to working on their own big ideas and innovations.) If a company wants people to behave differently, it may have to encourage that new behavior by changing the rewards and recognition policies in order to give people incentives to try new things or embrace new approaches. And it also may be necessary to implement structural changes, breaking down silos or dismantling some of the internal bureaucracy that may have been keeping the company from living up to its own ideals.

Mahindra has many faces but one soul. The Mahindra "Rise" movement was designed to spotlight and reward examples of people using innovative thinking—both inside and outside the company. So the company had to rethink some of its corporate policies to provide more opportunities and incentives for people throughout the company to experiment and try to innovate. The global program started in India with the launch of a multimedia campaign called "Spark the Rise," urging people to rise to the challenges all around them by posting ideas online. Ideas could be submitted in the areas of technology, energy, agriculture, infrastructure, transportation, and social entrepreneurship. Each month, the eight best ideas—as selected by public voting and a jury of experts—received funding from Mahindra, resulting in a total of 48 funded projects over the first six months of the program. A designated number of people employed at Mahindra were eligible to submit ideas, and virtually everyone connected with the company—including retailers and other business partners—became involved in the movement on some level. The "Rise" philosophy extends throughout a number of areas of the company, including recruitment and employee induction processes. (In job interviews, for example, the company began placing more emphasis on listening to the interviewee and paying special attention to a candidate's ability to focus on unmet needs of the customer and consider diverse viewpoints.) In terms of the movement's influence on the corporate culture, Mahindra's Ruzbeh Irani says, "Rise is the 'red thread' that connects the diverse businesses" of Mahindra; it is "fundamental to who we are."

I don't think a program as ambitious as this could ever have gotten off the ground without complete buy-in from the people in the company—who, by the time of the launch, were on board and ready to start spreading the movement. In the era of social media, a million Mahindra employees can conceivably touch many millions of connections. One person can put a video of his or her own "Rise" idea on YouTube and get 20,000 likes. Conversely, if those employees are not on board with the idea and the overall values of the movement, they can (perhaps unwittingly) undermine the movement in some small way. These days, any employee can make a comment on Facebook that contradicts the idea you're trying to put out there.

CHANGE THE WAY PEOPLE FEEL ABOUT THEIR OWN COMPANY

But in the end, this is about more than getting your employees to help promote a marketing idea. I think one of the most exciting aspects of movement marketing is the potential it offers for helping to change the way people think and feel about their own companies. Traditional ad campaigns, for the most part, can't do that because even if the ads themselves are fun and inspiring, they don't directly engage or involve the whole company, the way a movement can. An ad is unlikely to shift the culture of a company, or change the way people think about their jobs. But a movement can do this.

A great example (which our agency had no involvement with) was a campaign/movement started a few years ago by the Pedigree pet food brand, working with its agency, TBWA/Chiat/Day in Los Angeles. Agency creative chief Lee Clow—who, as previously mentioned, was an integral figure in helping to shape not just Apple's advertising, but the "Think Different" movement that reinvigorated Apple's corporate culture in the late 1990s—also helped usher in a cultural transformation at Pedigree. Clow says it all began when TBWA challenged the brand to "figure out what they believe, as opposed to what they sell."

Pedigree believed in dogs—the company's history, which had long focused on improving the training, the diet, and the lives of canines, bore that out. And Clow felt that Pedigree was well positioned to lead a movement championing dogs' rights and rallying the support of dog lovers everywhere. But first the company had to make a strong declaration of its position on dogs, and it had to change its own culture to be much more dog-centric. It started with the creation of a manifesto that became the basis of a company handbook titled "Dogma," which laid out a new Pedigree philosophy, summed up in the line "we're for dogs."

"Dogma" was intended to tell employees that it was "a new day" at the company; meanwhile, the words were backed up by actions and policy changes. The company changed the culture by implementing dog-friendly policies in its own workplace, encouraging associates to bring their dogs to work (creating ID badges and business cards that featured pictures of employees' dogs) and even extending health-care benefits to associates' dogs. As the movement eventually went from the inside of the company to the outside world, Pedigree took some bold actions to demonstrate its commitment to championing the cause of dogs. The company launched an initiative encouraging people to adopt homeless dogs, and even built a pop-up dog store in Times Square featuring a dog adoption center. Meanwhile, the company's ads promoted the shelter initiative, while the Pedigree website became a dog lovers' gathering spot, where dog stories and photos could be swapped. Pedigree even went so far as to declare and promote an international holiday for dogs.

The "Dogs Rule" movement was deemed a success, both from a purely business standpoint (it boosted sales and burnished Pedigree's image as a company that cares about dogs) and in terms of the significant contributions it made to helping dogs in shelters. But maybe its most important accomplishment was to transform the Pedigree culture in a way that had a profound effect on the people who worked there. As Clow noted, the people at Pedigree "used to come to work every day thinking they worked for a dog food company. Now they come in thinking they work for a company that loves dogs. That's a huge difference."

If you look at the companies that are leading the most successful brand movements, you'll find that in many cases, they have developed and fostered a culture of "true believers" inside the company. It's true at Apple, at Nike (the everyday athletes at Nike are the perfect ambassadors for a movement that attempts to rouse and inspire the athlete inside all of us, employing that now-classic rallying cry, "Just Do It"), and more recently at Zappos, a company whose near obsession with developing a strong culture has been central to its ability to attract loyal followers in the highly competitive online marketplace. In business today, having the right culture in place is a critical component of success—it's hard to stand for something positive to the outside world if you don't also stand for the same kinds of values inside the company. Having a disconnect between inside and outside will sap energy from any kind of movement or initiative you're trying to launch. And ultimately it will undermine your credibility—because if you don't think the world out there is paying attention to everything you do as a company, then you haven't been paying attention to what's going on in the transparent business environment of today.

MOVE FROM INSIDE TO OUTSIDE

Once you've established an internal culture to support a movement, you're well on your way—but you're still not quite ready to launch your movement. You've got your own in-house community (your company) on board, but the movement will eventually have to move beyond your walls, coming to life in an outside community of people who are inclined to embrace the idea you're championing.

Chances are that this community already exists—you don't have to build it or create it. Somewhere out there are people who care about X, who are passionate about Y, or who are downright obsessed with Z. This is not some vague "18 to 54" marketing demographic; it will tend to be a much more defined group, united around a shared interest or passion.

THE KEY STEPS TO COMMUNICATING A MOVEMENT IDEA

At StrawberryFrog, we've broken down the communications planning steps into the following approach:

- Align with a powerful idea on the rise to define a culture
- Create content/actions/tools/events/communities to draw people to this idea
- Start in places where conversations are already happening
- Recruit your most outspoken advocates
- Use mass communications to amplify to a wider audience
- Curate the idea by using search engine optimization
- Activate word of mouth with PR, social media, and content placement
- Invent ownable media in online and offline channels to continue the conversation
- Use direct marketing and promotions to encourage purchase

If you compare movements to advertising, here are the differences: Movements are sustainable; rooted in passion; multiplatform; others talking about you; inspiring behavior and new habits; open to many.

Advertising has a beginning and an end, it interrupts people; is typically rooted in product and traditional media; it talks about itself; influences behavior; and is exclusive. Traditional agencies always default to mass communications first, while some think one step further. Last year during the Super Bowl, VW launched "The Force" Star Wars inspired TV spot online for the first time, before it was seen during the game, gathering phenomenal momentum and fans long before it broke on TV.

These people are not hard to find. They gather around blogs, websites, Facebook groups, clubs, organizations, and events having to do with the issue(s) they care about. The most vocal and influential among them are tracked by "seeding companies" that build massive black books of bloggers and vloggers. We sometimes work with these seeding companies to build our initial lists of "key influencers" that we want to reach out to first. But even without access to a seeding specialist, you can find these influencers fairly easily. If you're doing a movement that has to do with helping people get out of bed in the morning, you'll probably find a Facebook group called "I hate getting up in the morning," and that's a good place to start.

The challenge is not so much locating the interested communities for any movement idea—it's figuring out how to connect with them in effective ways. For the most part, they're not interested in marketing pitches or press releases or anything that reeks of promotion. A lot of marketers try to buy bloggers with freebies and giveaways, but from our experience, we find most of them don't want to be bought. So what are they looking for? Authentic ideas and content that they can actually use. They want your story—but only if it's an interesting one, a meaningful or useful one, and therefore one worth sharing with the community.

What you must do, then, is make sure the story you're trying to tell fits these criteria. Will it be of interest to the people in this community? Will it be of any use to them? The best way we've found to ensure this is by following a two-pronged approach:

1. Start by making sure you really understand the community you're trying to reach—its interests, needs, goals, habits, and so on.

2. Then focus on your message to make sure it has the qualities and characteristics that will appeal to this group.

GET INSIDE THE MINDS AND HEARTS OF THE COMMUNITY

Research is critical to helping you understand how to talk to the community you're trying to reach. When I say the word *research*, I don't necessarily mean the typical marketing research approaches and tools: focus groups, surveys, and studies. Those conventional tools can be useful, but I think movement marketing calls for a more direct and "human" approach to research. For that reason, we do a lot of ethnographic work, going into people's homes or the places (both virtual and real) where they spend time with their friends. As much as possible, we try to immerse ourselves in their world. And we rely on deep observation and listening to try to get beneath the surface in understanding why people are passionate about certain issues.

Having this kind of up-close contact with a community can help you sharpen the thrust and message of the movement, while also providing clues on the best ways to deliver that message. What are these people's frustrations? What do they want to change? On a more practical level, how do they receive and exchange information? Do they like certain types of entertainment? Are they heavy users of particular forms of social media? All of that can help inform your efforts to reach them.

The research can also provide great individual stories that can sometimes be picked up and incorporated into the larger movement story. In a recent campaign for Sharpie markers, created by the brand and its agency, Draftfcb, the company spotlights customers that it discovered were doing extremely creative things with the brand's markers (customizing skateboards, writing songs, turning coffee cups into works of art), and this formed the basis of a brand movement urging people to "Start Something" by using the markers to express their creativity in original ways. This was not unlike our own experience in the previously mentioned movement that we did for the True North brand, in which the stories of passionate baby boomers pursuing their second-act life dreams gave us wonderful raw material to build our communications around. But the point is, you have to go out and really talk to people—and step into their worlds—in order to be able to dig out these stories and insights about their lives.

COMPELLING AND USEFUL: WHAT MAKES MOVEMENT IDEAS APPEALING

Now that you've done the research, it's time to shift your focus to the communications—the basic messaging you'll be putting out there into the world as you try to connect with this community of people that you'd like to eventually mobilize. Everything you put out there should reflect these people's interests and needs. It should be original and creative. It should represent the brand well. It should be a lot of things, but to break it down to the two most important characteristics, everything you put out there should be both compelling and useful.

And with this in mind, you need to understand that conventional advertising may not, and probably shouldn't, play a dominant role in your messaging. Conventional ads are only rarely compelling and almost never useful. A commercial—if it's done right, and captures the spirit of a movement in a truly compelling and motivating way—can sometimes be used as an initial rallying cry or a way to reinforce some of the other outreach efforts involved in developing a movement. But overall, the messaging that drives any good movement should extend way beyond advertising, taking many forms of communication that are more direct, more tailored to the movement, and more relevant to people's lives than advertising. The bad news for marketers is that this can be more challenging than just making an ad. The good news is that today there are countless ways to create content that do not involve making ads: everything from web films to apps, from platforms you create to events you organize, and even encompassing things that are hard to categorize, such as novelty items, comic books— you name it. The content you share with the community can take just about any form, but what matters is that it be compelling and useful—because that, in turn, will tend to make it shareable.

I talked briefly about "swarm theory" in Chapter 4, and I want to return to that here just to make a point about why certain things tend to get noticed, picked up, and shared by a community. In a swarm (of, let's say, bees), the swarm is always on the lookout for threats and opportunities, which can influence the direction the swarm moves in—but whatever that outside stimulus may be, it has to be *compelling* or attractive enough to catch the attention of the swarm. Members of the swarm may also pick up and share something (food, for instance) that is *useful* to the group. In the same way, communities of people—who don't travel in actual swarms, but who do engage in similar swarming and sharing behaviors on Facebook or Twitter, or at real-world gatherings and events—are also on the lookout for something that is compelling or useful enough that it warrants being passed along to other members of the group.

This raises the question: what are members of the group likely to consider compelling or useful? Let's start with the "useful" part first, because this really is a foreign concept for most marketers. Of course, marketers are accustomed to trying to attract attention (that's been a fundamental requirement of advertising all along), but most people on the marketing/advertising side have little experience when it comes to putting something out there in the world that is actually *useful*. I'm not talking here about the product or service a company is offering, which, hopefully, is useful in some way; I'm talking about all the things that are created and disseminated as part of promoting that product. From the consumer's standpoint, all of that messaging coming at him or her may be annoying, amusing, or somewhere in between—but it's hardly ever useful. However, it doesn't have to be that way.

TAP INTO YOUR ASSETS

In terms of the ways marketers communicate and engage with consumers, there are lots of opportunities to be useful to people in general, and there are particular ways to be useful to a community or a burgeoning movement. One of the best ways to do this is to figure out how some of the company or brand's "assets" can be leveraged to meet the needs that exist out there.

Douglas Atkin, a former top executive at Meetup.com and an author who's written extensively on brands and communities, observes that one of the chief ways in which brands can "attract followers who will spread your brand gospel" is to, in Atkin's words, "enable a community of shared needs." Or, to put it more simply: "Be useful to people who want or need to share stuff," Atkin writes.

What can you offer that might be useful to a community?

- **EXPERTISE.** Your company can share your inside knowledge about a subject that may be of interest to the community. When we did the Boomer Coalition for Pfizer, the company was able to share the health and medical information that the audience was looking for, while in the case of Pampers, the brand could offer much-needed parenting advice and resources.

- **CONNECTING PLATFORMS.** Community members often need a place to gather, and companies are in a good position to provide that (the site Pampers Village is a good example).

- **CONTENT.** This includes everything from short web films that can be passed around to stories that can run on key influencers' blogs. The key here is to become a curator of content for the community, finding and selecting the kind of material that's most relevant and interesting.

- **TOOLS.** This could include anything you can offer that can make people's lives a little easier or more interesting. For example, a company can create free or inexpensive apps that solve a problem for people. (Pampers has done this with parenting apps, while our Microsoft small business client provided free small business software to core members of the "Idea Wins" movement.)

- **EVENTS.** For a number of our movements, including the Boomer Coalition, we've organized concerts and other events as a way to bring the community together, generate enthusiasm, pass out movement-themed swag, and so on.

The goal is to use your company's assets any way you can to create "commons"—those shared resources that your brand offers as a means of helping people connect with one another and advance the goals of a movement. This is one of the best ways to begin to forge an authentic bond between the brand and a community.

While it's critical to offer the community something useful, it's just as important to make sure that every piece of messaging you put out there is compelling. What makes content compelling? Different people may have different answers to that question, but I think whatever you share should be smart, fresh, surprising, and either funny or moving in some way. Marketers may be used to applying such creative standards to big-budget commercials, but you have to do likewise with everything from web films to apps—everything you provide should pass the same high-level engagement standards. Basically, everything you share with the community should be able to pass a basic test, in the form of this question: why would anyone care about this?

Before you actually release your message to the public— whether by seeding it among influential bloggers or starting with more of a big, mass-audience debut—I think it's important that you plan out in advance the desired progression of events. What we like to do is "write the narrative" of a movement we're trying to spark before it actually begins. The idea is to document it as if it were a case study of something that has already happened: *we launched it this way, then these people heard about it and got involved by doing X, then it quickly spread to Y, and we reacted by doing Z.* Of course you should do this knowing that with movements, nothing is likely to go exactly as planned.

BE PURPOSELY PROVOCATIVE

One thing to be prepared for is the possibility that as you begin to put your movement idea out there into the world, it may be tough, initially, to get people to pay attention. That doesn't necessarily mean that the idea isn't a worthy one—just that it's hard to break through when there is so much competing for people's attention these days (including lots of other movements!). To get on the radar, you may have to do what we refer to as a provocation.

A provocation is exactly what it sounds like: an attempt to get people's attention by doing something unexpected, extreme, and perhaps even a little bit risky. If you think about the nature of movements—and this includes all types of social and cultural movements, as well as brand movements—they often seem to gain that first rush of momentum because of some provocative action that manages to draw attention and galvanize people around an issue.

Examples of this can be seen in both historical social movements and some of the newer uprisings that have been making news of late. For example, starting in mid-2011, Israel was rocked by a series of "social justice" protests decrying the country's difficult economic conditions, including high costs of food and education and a lack of affordable housing. The protests were far-flung and built up gradually over time, but one event that seemed to galvanize people and jet-boost the movement was a simple, provocative act: in Tel Aviv, a small group of friends set up tents downtown to protest housing prices.

Meanwhile, at roughly the same time, a massive anticorruption movement was springing up in India. Obviously there were many factors that led up to the protests, but what really lit the fire was the action of a 74-year-old man named Anna Hazare. Inspired by Gandhi, Hazare staged a hunger strike at a park in New Delhi, demanding that the government create an anticorruption agency. Instead, the government arrested him, which caused an immediate uproar. Seeing its mistake, the Indian government quickly tried to release him—but Hazare refused to come out of jail, continuing his fast there.

MOVEMENT HELPING IMPOVERISHED WOMEN

EXEMPLAR HALF THE SKY

THE BIG IDEA Half the Sky offers a call to action for people to join the movement to emancipate women and fight global poverty by unlocking women's power as economic catalysts. A main aim of Half the Sky is to get individuals and policy makers to ask the necessary questions and get the key issues, such as human trafficking, on their agendas. The movement does not do fund-raising itself, but rather members are directed to lists of causes and groups they can support.

STARTED Nicholas D. Kristof and Sheryl WuDunn founded Half the Sky in September 2009.

HOW IT SPREAD   Half the Sky started with a best-selling book of the same name by Pulitzer Prize winners Nicholas Kristof (*New York Times* columnist) and his wife, journalist Sheryl WuDunn. The book and the companion website outline inspiring efforts by individuals and organizations, Westerners and locals, social entrepreneurs, medical professionals, and ordinary citizens, and they direct supporters to long lists of groups that specialize in supporting women in developing countries. The site's focus on storytelling helps to bring the women's issues to life.

WHERE IT STANDS NOW   Kristof has a huge social media following (more than 1 million on Twitter) and a journalistic platform that keeps the movement front and center for his followers. Several nonprofit organizations mentioned in *Half the Sky* have produced additional events and materials in support of the book, including a live event by the relief agency CARE.

QUOTE   "We really want people to move from being upset as they read the book to being engaged in these causes. At the end of the book we list four things people can do in the next ten minutes—the afterword lists a bunch of organizations that are doing great work—and we want people not just to be check writers but also to be volunteers, to go visit a project they may have adopted, and to actually spend time in the grass roots. It is a transformative experience."—Nicholas D. Kristof, founder

WEBSITE   Halftheskymovement.org

Social movements tend to bring out these acts of individual heroism, which then inspire others. In the more mundane (and far less dangerous) world of marketing, no one needs to show the kind of courage that Anna Hazare showed. However, marketers who are looking to inspire followers may need to show a willingness to take a bit of heat in order to draw attention to their cause at the outset. A case in point is a small movie theater chain based in Austin, Texas, that recently started its own movement to get people to behave in theaters. The Alamo Drafthouse Cinema took an unusually strong stand against those who talk, text, read e-mails, and engage in other distracting behaviors during movies. Many of the theater's customers supported this idea and rallied around it—but it didn't *really* get on the radar until the theater's chief executive, Tim League, did something provocative.

After a customer who'd been ejected from the theater for texting left a complaining message on the theater's answering machine—and it helped that the message was both rambling and ridiculous, with the caller apparently believing that she had *every right* to annoy other moviegoers by texting in the theater— League took that obnoxious message and went public with it, playing it on his screens and even putting it on YouTube. There was an element of risk in doing this; he opened himself up to possible criticism for playing a private message or for making fun of an angry customer. But most people were tickled by the recording, and it soon went viral, drawing more than 4 million views on YouTube. Soon, the Alamo Drafthouse's modest movement to bring quiet to theaters was being discussed in national news reports and opinion shows (clearly, the local theater had seized upon an idea that was already "on the rise" among theatergoers across the country).

In our own movement marketing efforts, we've employed various provocations to get things jump-started. As noted in the previous chapter, we launched Microsoft's small business software program, and the entrepreneurial movement built around it, by dropping software from the sky in parachutes. It was an action that was just odd and baffling enough to get the media asking, "What's going on here?" and thus our movement had some early attention and momentum.

In this age of social media, YouTube in particular, it's easier than ever before to get something provocative out there. Create a short film that gets people talking—and that particularly speaks to the concerns of your core group—and your movement can quickly be up and running.

When we were launching the idea of a "Bold Choice" movement for Jim Beam, a two-minute film we created featuring the actor Willem Dafoe drew widespread attention because of unusual elements in the film (Dafoe was almost unrecognizable as he morphed into several different characters) and a controversial ending to the vignette. It should be noted, though, that the film was true to the spirit and message of the movement we were trying to launch. Whatever provocation you choose, be sure that it doesn't come across as off-message and that it doesn't somehow undercut the point of the movement.

THE IMPORTANCE OF HAVING FUN

One thing we've found is that while there is a serious aspect to movements—you may be trying to put forth an important idea or rally people to do something meaningful—it always seems to help if you can inject elements of playfulness, humor, outrageousness, and just plain fun into movements wherever possible. We can all learn a lot from the folks behind the movement Improv

Everywhere, which brings people together to stage public pranks (see the movement profile in Chapter 7).

The use of pranks and stunts (including everything from public pie fights to the recent phenomenon *du jour* known as the flash mob) can be a great tool for attracting attention, of course. But perhaps more important, it can help promote a spirit of mischievous fun that can energize the members of a movement and bring them closer together.

This brings up another point: movements thrive on a sense of *togetherness*, which is best achieved through human contact—the kind that results when people gather for events, pranks, shared endeavors, or activities. When we arranged rock concerts as part of our Boomer Coalition movement, it became a great way to bring our core believers together, let them get to know one another, and have some fun. And if you're inclined to give out some cool movement-themed swag in the process, so much the better. This is important not just at the early, getting-to-know-you stages of a movement, but also later, when events can be a way to keep a movement feeling vital and authentic. Even in the digital age, there's no substitute for bringing people together in the public square.

In fact, it is particularly important to keep this in mind in this current age of so-called clicktivism, when it's seemingly possible to launch and even maintain a movement almost entirely in the digital realm. It may be true that you can get people to sign up for just about anything online these days, but the real measure of their involvement and commitment is whether they'll actually, physically, *show up* for something. The Occupy Wall Street movement probably wouldn't have had much impact if it all happened online; by "occupying" an actual, physical space, it became something that was hard to ignore.

So in light of that, it's a good idea to try to "make something happen" in the physical, real world as much as you can. Organize activities. Give people something to do together. A case in point is the movement started a couple of years back by the paint company Dulux, under the banner of "Let's Colour," which brought together groups of volunteers for the express purpose of going to dreary-looking parks and town squares and brightening things up with colorful fresh coats of paint. A bonus: these types of public happenings can be turned into inspiring content. You just film or document the event in some way, and you can then share it online with other members of the community who couldn't be part of the "live" event but still want to share in the spirit of being there.

SYMBOLS, FLAGS, AND YELLOW WRISTBANDS

As your movement begins to come together in the real world through actual participation at events, there are ways to foster and strengthen the human connection within the group. And one of the best ways to build unity within the group is through the use of shared symbols and totems.

Movement flags, T-shirts, banners, and the like have always been a part of movements; they're one of the key ways in which members of a movement begin to identify one another and feel like part of a club with its own look and language. And seeing the symbols of a movement surrounding you can have some interesting effects, as the designer Brian Collins has noted. Collins, who at one point worked on the logos and iconography for Al Gore's climate protection movement, observed, "Any movement has to have its own unique symbols and flags, to let people see it exists." As those symbols begin to appear all around, Collins says, "It can make the movement seem even bigger and more powerful." For example, Occupy Wall Street's raised-fist logo became a unifying symbol as the movement spread to other cities (in many cases, those cities adapted and customized the logo in some way to make it their own).

In terms of brand-related movements, it's hard to think of any that made better use of such symbolism than LIVESTRONG, the movement started by cycling legend and cancer survivor Lance Armstrong. Through his Lance Armstrong Foundation, and with support from Nike and other savvy marketing partners, Armstrong attracted millions of people to an endeavor that morphed from a charity to a mass movement of followers, with each member wearing a yellow wristband (more than 75 million of the wristbands have been sold, with all the proceeds going to support cancer survivors). The amazing rise of LIVESTRONG was no accident—as noted by one of the architects of the campaign to launch the wristband, the veteran marketing executive Marty Cooke, the initiative combined all the elements of a great movement, including a terrific cause, an inspirational leader, an iconic symbol, and some strong grassroots organization (see the sidebar on LIVESTRONG).

The LIVESTRONG campaign, by the way, not only offers a lesson in the power of symbols, but serves as a model for how a high-profile brand (in this case, Nike) can sometimes best partner with a movement by taking a low-key approach. Nike didn't put its name or swoosh symbol on the yellow wristbands; it allowed Armstrong and the cause to own the spotlight. "Nike let Lance be the face and force of the movement," says Cooke. Behind the scenes, the brand did a lot—it helped produce and pay for the wristbands, then used its sports marketing clout to make sure they were worn by many of its sponsored athletes. "They had the largeness of heart and vision to put their commercial interests on the back burner," Cooke says. Still, most people who know about LIVESTRONG also know that Nike is involved, so the brand has reaped major brand-image benefits, even while taking a soft-sell approach.

MOVEMENT CAUSE MARKETING

EXEMPLAR LIVESTRONG

THE BIG IDEA The LIVESTRONG movement serves as the voice of men and women who are affected by cancer, backing research projects and encouraging survivors to live life to the fullest. The LIVESTRONG yellow silicone wristbands started out as a fund-raising item designed by Nike and the Lance Armstrong Foundation and ended up becoming a wildly popular fashion accessory overnight.

STARTED LIVESTRONG was started in May 2004 by Lance Armstrong, seven-time Tour de France winner and cancer survivor, and Nike in a nonprofit marketing effort.

HOW IT SPREAD Lance Armstrong wore the LIVESTRONG band at the Athens Olympic Games. Following that appearance, journalist Katie Couric, Democratic presidential candidate John Kerry, and actor Matt Damon were seen sporting the band. Shortly after, satirical and comedy personalities incorporated their version of the band (*The Colbert Report*, Ben Stiller, *The Office*). The foundation's volunteers are crucial to its success, and there are constant walks, runs, rides, triathlons, and other local fund-raising events that encourage support and participation.

WHERE IT STANDS NOW LIVESTRONG has used its success to branch off into suicide support as well as specialized groups of cancer survivors—young adults, African Americans, and Native Americans.

QUOTE "We were all shocked by the impact of the wristband. LIVESTRONG as a concept really resonated with people and we realized we were on to something. . . . The brand took off and in turn brought more attention to the disease and the foundation."—Lance Armstrong, founder

WEBSITE Livestrong.org

You know you've made it as a mainstream cultural movement when you're being parodied—and everyone from Comedy Central anchor Stephen Colbert to comedian Ben Stiller has had some playful fun with LIVESTRONG and the yellow wristbands. (In Stiller's case, he created his own derivative mini-movement called "STILLERSTRONG," featuring yellow headbands instead of yellow wristbands. The blatant rip-off of Armstrong is played for laughs, although Stiller's cause is real: he's raising donations to help schoolkids in Haiti.)

When a movement has reached that level of recognition and success, a new set of challenges takes hold. It's no longer about "getting on the radar," but more about staying there. Once you've rallied people around an idea or a cause, how do you keep them interested and engaged? In the next chapter, we'll look at the keys to sustaining a movement and taking it to the next level. We'll also consider what happens when movements cross borders and go global, expanding from a local uprising to a worldwide phenomenon.

ORCHESTRATING SPONTANEITY: WHAT MADE THOSE YELLOW BRACELETS TAKE OFF?

As a former creative director at the marketing agency SS+K, which worked with the Lance Armstrong Foundation at the time of the LIVESTRONG bracelet launch, Marty Cooke was in the midst of one of the most successful brand-related uprisings ever. Here, Cooke shares some inside details on how the movement got started and took off.

"It was a perfect storm. Nobody expected it to become anything like what it turned out to be. [The idea of doing something with wristbands originated with Nike], but what the message on the band should be wasn't so obvious. At one point, Nike wanted to put its swoosh on it with the Latin phrase '*Carpe Diem*.' We felt strongly that the swoosh was wrong; it commercialized the wristband and, more important, it had nothing to do with cancer. Looking for a tagline for the movement, we had found, buried in the Lance Armstrong Foundation website, a small program called LIVESTRONG. It was the perfect message for the band, referring both to Lance's last name and his fighting attitude toward cancer.

"But why did this particular icon work so well? I think it had several powerful things going for it. First, nobody had ever seen a wristband for a cause. It was a new idea. New is good. Second, the LIVESTRONG message, tying back to Lance Armstrong, reflected his aggressive, 'take no prisoners' stance against cancer. This really resonated with people. The cancer community prior to Lance had been well-meaning and earnest, but the voice was subdued. Lance, on the other hand, was a brusque fighter—a rock-hard athlete who dominated the toughest competitive event in the world. The physical and mental toughness it took to win the Tour de France paralleled the toughness it took to defeat cancer. (The original version of the LIVESTRONG Manifesto ended with the phrase 'founded by one of the toughest motherfuckers on the planet.' Lance agreed with me, but the wiser heads of the foundation board asked us to soften it a bit.) I think the bold populism of the wristband was part of a countercultural undertone implicit in LIVESTRONG.

"The bright yellow color (originally chosen in honor of the yellow jersey worn by the winner of the Tour de France) of the bands attracted attention and engendered conversation: 'Why are you wearing Lance's band?' I think more than anything, being a conversation starter was the secret to its power. It got complete strangers talking. It united people in a completely democratic way.

"The first big exposure was in June of 2004 at the Cannes Film Festival. We managed to get the yellow wristband on a huge number of high-profile celebrities. Our invitation to the festival ("What Are You Wearing to Cannes?") contained the wristband, and all the stars at Cannes got one. Then came the Tour de France that summer—Lance and Nike got the wristband on the wrists of most of the Tour riders. Finally, in August, came the Summer Olympics, where Nike got hundreds of athletes to wear the yellow wristband. The movement went mass.

"By the fall, everybody who was anybody in the culture was wearing a LIVESTRONG wristband, including both presidential nominees.

"Not one penny was spent on paid media until sales reached 30 million. Up to that point, we just marveled at the numbers and the impact. But then we realized that all we were communicating was people's commitment to fighting cancer in the abstract. The band meant 'cancer' and not much more.

"But the foundation was committed to the cause of 'survivorship.' A survivor, in its lexicon, was anyone who *has* or *has had* cancer. When we reached that 30 million number, we did some research, which pointed out something we'd all noticed: behind every LIVESTRONG wristband was an incredible story of survivorship. Whether it was their own victory, their own continuing fight, or the story of a loved one, friend, or colleague who'd fought cancer, every wristband told a story.

"These were the stories of survivorship, so we invited people to 'Share Your Story' at a new LIVESTRONG website. People wrote in by the thousands. And the yellow wristband started to take on a bit more strategic direction. We started to underline that this was not just about a lot of individuals who'd made a donation. We linked the yellow wristbands together like a chain with the line 'Unity Is Strength.' Suddenly the individual statement was now a *movement*.

"There's a term we discovered a few years later working on the Obama campaign that describes this gentle nudging; it's called *orchestrating spontaneity*. It looks spontaneous and reactive to the members of the movement. But in actual fact, it's carefully planned, often weeks or even months in advance. Steering a popular movement requires a deft hand. Without it, a powerful movement runs the risk of splintering into meaninglessness."

TBWA'S LEE CLOW ON CREATING A CORPORATE CULTURE THAT CAN DRIVE A MOVEMENT

Lee Clow, the longtime creative chief at TBWA Worldwide, is known for helping to launch great brand movements for Apple Computer, Pedigree pet food, Pepsi, and others. Here, Clow discusses his belief that great movements often begin inside the company, where top executives must be willing to lead and implement a culture change.

"One of the things I believe strongly is that the way brands are judged in today's culture, there has to be a 'caring' part of the brand. The world has such an ability to see brands clearly now, because of the Internet and social media, that a brand can't have a false presentation to the world, and then operate behind the scenes in a contradictory way. The totality of the behavior of the brand is under scrutiny by the public. Everything a brand does is basically an ad now.

"Some companies, like Zappos and Ben & Jerry's, have no problem with this because they are actually built upon a 'we care about the world' mentality. But I think even companies that are more pragmatic businesses can make this kind of cultural shift. Pedigree's a good example.

"Pedigree was a dog food company. And we said to them, why shouldn't you build a culture that loves dogs? 'Everything we do is for the love of dogs' was the mantra I laid on the table. The idea was, 'Let's get out of the left-brain thinking that we're a dog food company and move to the right brain, where we can be a company that loves dogs.'

"Unfortunately, there are a lot more left-brained people at most companies than right-brained people. You take that word *love*—when we started using that word at Pedigree, it freaked people out. All these left-brain MBAs that came out of school with formulas for packaging and marketing and pricing—you throw *love* on the table and it scares the shit out of them. So there's a gauntlet you have to run to try to deliver an idea like this.

"Luckily the guy at the top [of Pedigree] liked the idea, but more important, he was willing to hold everyone's feet to the fire inside the company. He said, 'If we go down this path, we have to walk the walk.' He knew this couldn't just be a little charity gesture (because all companies do that to try to prove in a superficial way that they're good citizens). He knew that to do it right, Pedigree was going to have to change its culture in a number of ways. It started with producing the company book, *Dogma*, which said to everyone, 'This is how we behave as a company from now on.'

"When we introduced the ideas of Pepsi Refresh and Pedigree, we said to these companies, 'You need to create a movement because you're trying to get followers who believe what you believe. So you have to behave as if you believe in this thing and then ask people to wear the bracelet or the T-shirt and be part of the movement as well.' Many companies aren't willing to go far enough to make it into that sustainable movement. But if you only go halfway—if you treat the movement as just a little marketing promotion idea—people out there know it. They don't want to invest time, money, and energy into something that's just a façade—a false promise. So if you're going to make it a movement, you'd better make it a real one.

"I think the reality for every brand that wants to be embedded in the culture, and have the kind of cultural relevance that an Apple does, is that it has to decide that the totality of this brand and how it does business is going to be totally transparent. And it has to believe in what it's doing. Steve Jobs, from when I first met him, before the first Macintosh was ever launched—he always believed that technology was going to change the world, that it should make people's lives better. He was not just in the business of making money, and he was not a nerd who just loved the stuff computers could do—he really believed he was part of something world-changing. And that's why he was always dedicated to making it as accessible and easy to use as possible. And that became so embedded in that company—that we are going to make people's lives better, change how they live—that it was really the soul of the company."

CHAPTER 7

Sustaining a Movement—and Taking It Global

A few years ago, when we were working with Scion, Toyota's brand for the youth generation, we found that the Scion's customer base was very interested in customization of cars as a form of self-expression. We immediately saw a movement opportunity here: if we could somehow give these people the tools to customize their cars in interesting new ways, we'd be providing the kind of useful service that could strengthen their ties to the brand. But to make it a movement, we also needed to do something to tie these people closer together, to create a sense of shared identity. Our dream was to create a kind of underground car enthusiast movement that had its own distinct language and symbols. So we enlisted some graffiti artists to help us develop some stylish digital art templates, then built a website that enabled visitors to take these supplied graffiti art images and adapt them to create their own Scion symbols and crests. The crests could be placed on cars or displayed in any number of ways, so that the enthusiasts could recognize one another wherever they might meet, all the while feeling that they were part of something that was fresh and "under the radar."

That thrill of being involved in something that's new and a little mysterious, something that's just bubbling up and is understood or recognized only by savvy "insiders," is undeniably a big part of what gets people excited in the early stages as you're introducing a movement initiative. We generally do everything we can to encourage that feeling of "insider" status. When we first introduced this website and the whole idea of a new language of symbols that we called "Scion Speak," we gave the website password only to the more hard-core Scion fans, the true believers—we wanted them to be the ones talking about it, while others were on the outside looking in and wondering what these crests and this "language" were all about. It worked beautifully. Of course, somewhere along the way, this underground idea broke through to the mainstream: suddenly, the *New York Times* was writing about "Scion Speak." The site was now open to everyone and was drawing lots of visitors. The movement was branching out.

This is exactly what you want to happen with a brand movement, of course; it's the goal and the measure of success. Yet it also represents a great danger to a growing movement: that moment when something that was cool and underground, something that felt exclusive to people in the know, suddenly becomes something else—familiar, mainstream, and (quite literally, in the aftermath of the *Times* article) yesterday's news. At that point, it's no longer something that people can excitedly share with friends, because their friends already know about it.

This raises an interesting question that is one of the two focuses in this chapter: What happens after the launch of a movement? When you put an idea out there into the culture and people begin to gather around it, how do you keep things fresh, interesting, and moving ahead? Later in the chapter, we'll also take a look at what happens when a movement idea proves so sustainable and enlargeable that it begins to achieve global expansion and adoption. But first, let's start smaller and closer to home: how do you sustain a movement as it first begins to take hold and grow?

This may sound like a problem that anyone starting a movement would love to have. After all, it can be so hard to get on the radar initially with any kind of campaign or movement that people may assume that a cultural breakthrough of any kind is a total victory. But in some ways, it can be harder to sustain a movement than to start one. Often, people will take an early interest—just out of pure curiosity—in something that's fresh and novel. But movements can lose momentum as quickly as they gain it. And if that happens, it's a serious problem because one of the basic truisms about a movement—any type of movement, not just brand movements—is that if it stops "moving," it dies. If there isn't something new happening to stir people's interest and get them engaged, they'll tend to move on to the next thing that fires them up.

I used the term *provocation* in the previous chapter, advising that you have to do something noticeable to get on the radar. But the truth is, you really have to *keep on* provoking in order to *stay* on the radar. In a social movement, those outside provocations may come from forces on the other side—say, when authorities engage in a crackdown or put a movement leader in prison. Each new outrage fires up the movement once again, injects it with new energy, and keeps it going. With a brand movement, you may have to manufacture those new provocations on a regular basis. The good news is that they can involve relatively small actions and gestures (and you don't have to lock anybody up).

What you must do, however, is keep surprising people in some way. LIVESTRONG, as discussed in the last chapter, is a movement that has been living strong for more than a decade. The yellow wristbands were a phenomenon, of course—but even those amazing bracelets couldn't sustain the momentum indefinitely. There came a point when the wristbands were so omnipresent that people just kind of took them for granted. Yet the LIVESTRONG movement, on a fairly regular basis, keeps doing little things that pique members' interest and keep them engaged and involved.

One of the more recent was the "Chalkbot" experiment, developed with Nike, involving an odd-looking contraption that resembled a large ink-jet printer mounted on a trailer. In cycling, there is a tradition of using chalk to write inspirational messages to riders along the race course; the Chalkbot machine took this tradition to a new level by spraying messages—previously submitted by members of the public, using Twitter or the LIVESTRONG website—along the roads on the Tour de France course to inspire the riders. Each printed message was instantly photographed; that photo, along with GPS coordinates, was e-mailed back to the author of the message. More than 36,000 messages were posted, millions of dollars were raised, and marketing awards were bestowed. But while the idea was immensely clever, it wasn't anything big or flashy—it involved writing on the pavement in chalk, for heaven's sake!

THE BIG VALUE OF SMALL IDEAS

The point is, with a movement, quirky and small new ideas have great currency. For marketers, this means that you have to learn how to think small, in terms of coming up with lots of little ideas on a consistent, ongoing basis. A traditional ad campaign is all about thinking big; a few expensive commercials get produced and then are aired over and over again for an extended period of time. You don't have that luxury with a movement, as it requires continuous feeding: lots of ideas must be put out there on an ongoing basis. This requires a profound shift in the marketing approach, one that moves away from focusing only on "the big idea" (that one great advertising concept that we can get a lot of mileage out of) and focuses instead on constantly feeding the fire with fresh ideas, stories, and bits of content that can be timely, varied, and episodic. In our Onitsuka Tiger movement, we were constantly generating ideas that were released continuously, in a variety of forms; they were "small ideas," in a sense—comic books, little web films, quirky novelty items such as those cans of "Hero's Breath"—but they had a very large cumulative effect.

One big advantage of the small ideas approach is that you can try more things; you can start a lot of little fires and see which ones seem to catch, then fan those particular flames. It enables you to react to current events. In today's "fast culture," things change very quickly—every day, it seems, a new Internet meme takes over and is suddenly on everyone's lips—and by producing lots of fresh content, you can connect your movement to things that are unfolding in the culture at the moment.

MOVEMENT GLOBAL WOMEN'S EMPOWERMENT

EXEMPLAR WOMEN'S VOICES NOW

THE BIG IDEA Women's Voices Now aims to empower women in areas where they are denied equality and give voice to the struggle for civil, economic, and political rights. The nonprofit WVN provides an online arena where groups, foundations, and movements can come together to encourage social and cultural change for millions of women around the world.

STARTED Leslie Sacks, a Los Angeles art gallery owner, founded Women's Voices Now in January 2010.

HOW IT SPREAD WVN got a great deal of media coverage by starting up *Women's Voices from the Muslim World: A Short-Film Festival*, a traveling film competition featuring 98 short films from 40 different countries, also available for viewing on the movement's website. This multimedia forum relies heavily on the Internet to weave together information, events, opinions, and policies. WVN also used Kickstarter to raise funds to allow the far-flung moviemakers to attend the film festival.

WHERE IT STANDS NOW In its second year, WVN aims to continue to engage with an international audience and empower women to bring gender equality to local communities around the world.

QUOTE "I thought: How do we get the message out? Give voice back to the people? And I kept coming back to the Internet and movies. There is moderation, there is tolerance in the Muslim worlds, but it's being blocked by extremists."—Leslie Sacks, founder

WEBSITE Womensvoicesnow.org

It also keeps your messaging from quickly becoming stale and overly familiar. A lot of advertising in the past was predicated on the supposed power of repetition—hammering the same ideas over and over again to try to get them into people's heads. But today, the best marketers understand that *novelty* is actually what gets through to a savvy, media-empowered audience that is easily able to avoid familiar or uninteresting messages. Putting aside movements for a second, even ad campaigns are moving in the direction of more small ideas rather than one big idea. The highly successful Geico insurance ad campaign has multiple themes, alternating among the popular cavemen characters, the brand's gecko mascot, celebrity mock-endorsers, and "rhetorical question" scenarios ("Can Geico really save you 15 percent on insurance? Does Elmer Fudd have trouble with the letter R?"). The marketer and blogger Gareth Kay notes that in today's media environment, "The bigger a brand gets, the smaller it must act—because doing lots of small stuff makes a brand feel personal and gives it energy and momentum." This is particularly true with movement marketing, which needs to be fast and fresh at all times.

It's somewhat counterintuitive, but coming up with small ideas can be harder than the big idea approach simply because it demands constant creativity instead of just the occasional big burst. So how do you manage to create all those bits of content to put out there? One way is to share the workload with the community by inviting its members to co-create. In a number of our movements, including True North and Smart Car, we've invited members of the movement to share stories or participate in ways that help generate fresh ideas and content. In the case of Scion, mentioned earlier, we tapped into people's artistic skills to help create all those crests.

PLAYING THE ROLE OF CURATOR

Sharpie, the maker of markers that I mentioned briefly in the last chapter (it's not a client, but I think it's doing a great job at movement building), has really tapped into its community to get lots of great content. As the writer Douglas Atkin notes, the company "sees its role as a *curator.*" It brings together all the members of its communities (which include lots of artists, designers, and other creative types) via social media, then tries to inspire them to do creative things, using Sharpie pens. As Atkin notes, the company "formed the 'Sharpie Squad' of 20 select individuals from the community to help stimulate, curate, and connect the rest." The whole idea was to get people busy creating stuff, and as they did, Sharpie would feature it in all kinds of interesting ways. Recently, for example, the company did a "YouTube takeover," during which YouTube's home page was filled with drawings, doodles, poems, and just about anything else the brand's movement members had created using a Sharpie.

When you empower the community to help create content for the movement, two big purposes are served. You get much-needed help in generating fresh, relevant material to share. And, at the same time, you allow people to feel more emotionally invested and directly involved in the movement. The term *crowdsourcing* is on everybody's lips these days, but the idea behind that trendy term is nothing new to movements—they have always been co-created by the people involved in them.

MOVEMENT PARTICIPATORY PUBLIC PRANKS

EXEMPLAR IMPROV EVERYWHERE

THE BIG IDEA Call it "organized fun." The idea is to cause a scene in a public place that is a positive experience for everyone who witnesses it. The slogan for Improv Everywhere is "We Cause Scenes."

STARTED Charlie Todd founded Improv Everywhere in New York City in 2001.

HOW IT SPREAD Several of IE's stunts have landed it in the public eye. VH1's "40 Greatest Pranks" celebrated IE's U2 prank (it convinced a huge crowd that U2 was playing on a rooftop until police intervened) in New York City. YouTube has been a huge factor in spreading the successes of the group.

WHERE IT STANDS NOW Improv Everywhere has executed more than 100 missions involving tens of thousands of participants and has 900,000 followers on YouTube. Charlie Todd lectures at universities and colleges, and wrote a book called *Causing a Scene*.

QUOTE "Even if it's a noble cause we personally support, Improv Everywhere does not stage missions to draw attention to an issue. We are focused on creating comedy for comedy's sake and staging events that purposefully have no explicit reason behind them, other than the goal of spreading chaos and joy throughout the world." — Charlie Todd, founder

WEBSITE ImprovEverywhere.com

But there is a challenge that comes with allowing people to help you create and shape the movement: it requires giving up some control of the marketing process. In fact, this is a central issue that I discuss with all clients who are thinking of pursuing a movement-driven approach to their brands: you must accept that if you allow people to truly engage with your brands, to interact with them, and to build movements around them, they may sometimes say or do things that don't follow your marketing script. In advertising, everything is subject to your control and approval; out there in the real world, where movements live, people are going to do what they will. Any marketer associated with movements must be able to live with that reality, and adapt accordingly.

This is one reason why movement marketing has, in the past, tended to work better for smaller, more entrepreneurial companies. Larger, more bureaucratic companies generally are locked into the mindset that every aspect of brand management must be tightly controlled. The idea of giving up some portion of that control to outsiders and total strangers can be downright scary for a large, traditional corporation. Indeed, getting involved with movements represents "a fantastic leap of faith for big companies because it's contrary to all they've been taught about how you can control everything through focus groups and testing and research," says Guy Kawasaki. But as Kawasaki notes, what these companies are really clinging to is "the illusion of control." Kawasaki's point is that in today's marketing landscape, social media has already pretty much obliterated a company's ability to determine what people are saying about brands, or how they're engaging with marketing messages (sometimes they're co-opting and hacking those ads).

So in terms of brands being willing to give up control, Kawasaki concludes: "You can't give up something you don't have."

LEADING FROM BELOW AND FROM WITHIN

It's also important to understand that these days, you don't really "lead" a movement; you just get out of the way and let others lead. One of the more interesting aspects of movements in the new digital age is that they often don't have clearly identifiable leaders. This is true of even the big social movements that have been reshaping the Middle East. In Syria, for instance, protesters took to the streets and battled the government and its military forces week after week—doing it all "without organization, strategy, or leadership," the *Washington Post* noted. The assumption is that social media makes this possible; with Twitter and other forms of instantaneous communication, the tasks of coordinating and organizing activities can be shared by many. In today's movements, anyone and everyone can become a leader for a day. (This may not actually be an entirely new phenomenon: Steve Breyman, a Rensselaer Polytechnic Institute professor who has studied the history of social movements, points to a long tradition of "leaderless" movements. This type of movement is described as SPIN, or "segmentary, polycentric, and integrated networks," which basically refers to movements that are very loosely formed, with constantly changing dynamics, including multiple, interchangeable leaders. The phenomenon was first cited in a book that is 40 years old, Breyman noted.)

It seems that the real breakthrough model for bottom-up, self-organizing movements in the digital era came in the political campaigns leading up to the 2008 U.S. presidential election, starting with Howard Dean's campaign in the Democratic primaries and culminating with Barack Obama's successful run for the presidency. The Obama campaign, in particular, understood that by dispersing responsibilities widely, and, more important, by extending them downward to the grassroots level, it not only would expand its reach, but would also give everyday people a real stake in the campaign—a true sense of belonging.

The campaign did a masterful job of using social media to connect supporters and rally them to take action. Using some of the money that would normally be spent on expensive TV commercials, it created a social network (my.obama.com) where supporters could organize events and connect with one another. Major responsibilities were handed off to people at all levels, with volunteers and grassroots supporters being given the kind of access and authority normally reserved for campaign higher-ups. The campaign encouraged people to set up their own local chapters and become self-appointed local campaign managers. It trusted volunteers enough to turn over precious voter lists to them, so that they could contact people directly; it also trusted them to do critical tasks like fund-raising (normally handled by rich and powerful campaign insiders). The result of all this was that Obama's campaign morphed from a campaign into an actual movement. And in so doing, it generated high levels of passion and engagement among many people, and ultimately did what movements are supposed to do—ushered in change.

What Obama did in the campaign offers lessons that go far beyond politics, extending to basically anyone trying to build a community. The folks at Meetup.com, which formed a decade ago as a movement designed to encourage people to use online technology to organize more offline gathering and socializing, are big believers in the notion that the only way to build and maintain strong communities is to delegate authority and share responsibility. Scott Heiferman, the cofounder of Meetup, advises that in order to use technology to harness the collective power of communities, you must do the following:

- Give people the power to self-organize and connect to each other.

- Give them something to do.

- Distribute responsibility.

- Set up situations that create opportunities for individuals to take responsibility and become leaders.

MOVEMENT **LOCAL COMMUNITY NETWORKING**

EXEMPLAR   MEETUP

THE BIG IDEA   Meetup's goal is to revitalize local communities and help people around the world self-organize by using the Internet to set up and run local offline groups. The movement's ultimate goal is a meetup everywhere about almost everything.

STARTED   Scott Heiferman, Matt Meeker, and Peter Kamali founded Meetup in New York City in June 2002, following a revelation after 9/11 that it's good to meet and know your neighbors. In the movement's early days, they tried charging the venues a fee; now they make money by charging meeting organizers $19 a month.

HOW IT SPREAD Meetup has never had a PR department. From the beginning, because of its founders' backgrounds in Internet start-ups, it was especially popular with techies, but it soon grew beyond that world. Early on, Heiferman did direct marketing outreach to numerous niche online groups, informing them of a made-up holiday—such as International Pug Lovers Meetup Day—and telling them to go to the Meetup website for their local meeting. This campaign was met with immediate enthusiasm by the groups (and today, for example, there are 40,000 members of 184 Pug Meetup groups around the world). In 2004, Meetup got the nascent Howard Dean campaign to use its website for organizing meetings; when the Dean campaign took off at a grassroots level in an unprecedented way, it garnered huge media attention for Meetup.

WHERE IT STANDS NOW Many a local movement has started up via Meetup, and 2010 was the first year with a million Meetups. In 2011, just under 10 million people had signed up and formed more than 90,000 local Meetup Groups in 45,000 cities. In 2010, the company launched Meetup Everywhere, a free widget to encourage impromptu meetups, which is being promoted by companies such as Huffington Post, Mashable, Foursquare, Etsy, TechCrunch, and YouTube.

QUOTE "Every Meetup starts with people simply saying hello to neighbors. And what often happens next is still amazing to me. They grow businesses and bands together, they teach and motivate each other, they babysit each other's kids and find other ways to work together. They have fun and find solace together. They make friends and form powerful community. It's powerful stuff." —Scott Heiferman, cofounder

WEBSITE Meetup.com

At StrawberryFrog, we've found that by letting others lead the movements we've started—encouraging them to set up their own mini-groups or Facebook pages and giving them platforms so that they can connect with others in the movement and plan initiatives or activities—the effect is to make the movements more self-sustaining. (However, it doesn't lessen the need to constantly keep "feeding" the movements with new ideas and provocations.)

We've also found that it's very important to listen closely (primarily through social media) to what the members of a movement are saying at all times. Over time, as people are involved with an idea or a cause, their feelings about it change, and their goals and ambitions may change. As this happens, you have to be willing to shift the movement in new directions, and to even question the fundamentals upon which you built it. Does the original idea still make sense? Has the culture shifted in a way that might cause you to want to rethink the idea a bit?

It may become necessary to reboot the movement by introducing an entirely new initiative, either to replace the original one or to add to it. I was impressed by TOMS Shoes' recent expansion of its movement. As previously described, TOMS was originally all about shoes, using a one-for-one model to donate a pair of shoes to poor kids for every pair sold. Now TOMS has extended the model to include eyeglasses—again, donating one pair of glasses for every pair sold. It's a way not only to add a product line to the business, but also to bring fresh energy to the TOMS movement by linking it to a whole new mission and worthy cause, this time involving kids' vision needs.

THE NEED FOR "QUIET TRANSPARENCY"

If a brand is involved in a movement, one of the most important things you must strive to build and maintain is trust. People today, whether because they're so savvy about marketing or because they're so connected by the Internet to what's going on in business and the world, have an uncanny knack for detecting any signs of insincerity or inconsistency on the part of brands. They watch what companies are doing very closely, and they watch a business even more closely when it is aligning itself with a cause or a movement. They look for signals that you're "walking the walk." But they don't necessarily want to hear you "talk the talk"—they're likely to be turned off if you overhype your involvement with a movement or cause.

This means that companies must practice what the futurist Bob Johansen described to me as "quiet transparency." It's a delicate balance between not hiding what you're doing, but not trumpeting it too much, either. If you support a movement, you should do it proudly and publicly—but don't brag about it or make a lot of self-congratulatory ads about it. That can create the impression that you're simply using the movement for PR spin purposes.

If you happen to be part of a large, multibrand company, be aware that people may be monitoring *all* your brands to see if they live up to the movement ideals espoused by *one* of your brands. A few years back, Unilever found itself dealing with complaints that it was preaching one movement philosophy on behalf of the Dove brand (which championed the "Real Beauty" movement described in Chapter 2) and then contradicting that with its marketing for Axe products, which was directed at young men and featured highly sexualized images of women. In an earlier time, consumers might never have connected the dots between those two separate brands, but today, they have access to all kinds of information about what a company and its various brands are doing. So the bottom line is, don't get caught doing something that goes against your movement's principles. If you do, you may quickly find that the movement has stopped trusting you—or, worse, that it has actually turned its forces *against* you.

One final thought about sustaining movements: from my own experience, brand movements often die not because the public got tired of them, but rather because the company lost faith or interest in the effort too quickly. At the time of this writing, there is evidence that this may be happening with the Pepsi Refresh Project, which did a great job of winning over the community but seems to have been less effective in winning over top management. (Pepsi sales were sluggish during the first year of Refresh; of course, it was a tough year overall in the soft drink business, and it should also be considered that the movement, at least initially, was understandably more focused on building trust and goodwill than on selling cans of Pepsi.)

For movements to get past some of the initial difficulties and adjustments involved, I think there has to be a complete buy-in from the company's top management. And the movement has to be seen as a deep corporate initiative, not just a marketing campaign. This brings us back to the previous chapter's discussion of corporate culture and why a movement must be ingrained in that culture in order to succeed and endure in the outside world. Marketing campaigns are temporary things that change with the wind or the latest sales numbers (or as soon as the new brand manager comes aboard). But if a movement idea or philosophy is embedded in the culture *inside* a company, then it may be able to survive long enough to effect change in the culture *outside* the company.

TAKING MOVEMENTS GLOBAL

In terms of getting top management at large companies to commit to a movement strategy, it's never been easy, but it is getting slightly easier—and I think there's a compelling reason why. Global companies are starting to realize that the world has changed in a way that is likely to have a profound impact on global brand marketing. People in different countries are now connected in ways they weren't before; they're sharing ideas and attitudes across borders. This presents a huge opportunity to create bona fide global marketing initiatives. I'm not talking about the old version of the so-called global campaign, where every country seemed to have its distinct way of promoting the same brand. What big brands have long hoped for but seldom achieved is a much more cohesive, integrated marketing strategy based on a universal theme that travels well from one country to the next. I think technology provides the first step toward making this happen; movements can provide the second.

Let's start with the changes wrought by technology. To a great extent, borders and boundaries have ceased to exist, as people tweet, blog, and chat online in real time, all the time, with just about every country on the planet. Facebook has practically become its own world, and the only border is the one that separates those who are connected from those who aren't. (In fact, there is interesting research suggesting that today, young people from different countries who are engaged in the digital realm are in many ways more similar and more connected to each other than they are to fellow countrymen who are not digitally engaged.) These digital platforms, such as Facebook, Google Plus, and LinkedIn, provide a great opportunity for global brands to connect with this new digital planet—if brands can earn their place in the global conversation.

A growing number of global marketers recognize that this is a seminal moment, one that demands a new way of approaching their task. "Before it was more of a global coordination as opposed to global management," noted Massimo F. d'Amore, CEO of Pepsi Beverages Americas, in a recent article in *Advertising Age*. "Technology, both social networks and mobile platforms, have created this global generation." The idea, says d'Amore, is to find well-orchestrated and well-managed ways to connect with that "global generation."

Advertising may not be the best way to do this (unless the ads are those rare exceptions that end up being universally loved and treated as shareworthy content). On the other hand, movement ideas—based on important, highly relevant themes that resonate with the ways in which people around the world are living today—have a better chance of working their way into the global idea exchange.

THE RISE OF THE "GLOBALISTAS"

This is not to suggest that everybody around the world is likely to respond to a given movement idea in the same way; there are still strong cultural differences that influence people's attitudes and views, of course. But today, much more than in the past, there is a real crossover of ideas and attitudes, particularly among the group of people that we tend to think of as the "globalistas." This relates to a phenomenon that we, as an agency, began to notice and document several years ago: we felt there was a new universal mindset emerging, a current made up of people and ideas circling the globe. We found that people were more likely than ever before to be interested in, and influenced by, ideas from other cultures.

The phenomenon seems to be strongest among the millennials. Born after the globalization boom, they have a much more unitary and integrated vision of the world. They tend to want to participate actively in other cultures, rather than just watch, visit, or read about them. And today they are contributing to a kind of great mosaic forming in the popular culture, made up of random bits and influences from all over the world. In fact, a number of our movements have been aimed squarely at this new multicultural mindset. StrawberryFrog's new global movement for Emirates Airline is based on this insight. Emirates is on its way to becoming the biggest airline in the world and our work for them (which launches in early 2012) taps into the idea of a new "globalista" movement.

Interestingly, this global mindset is also starting to take hold within many top companies, where a new generation of leaders hailing from many different countries is coming to the fore. Increasingly, these top executives are people with culturally diverse backgrounds; they may have grown up in one country, been educated in another, and now find themselves stationed in yet another. They circle the globe regularly, they're open-minded about all cultures, and their influences and inspirations tend to be drawn from all over the place.

These new business leaders are also keenly aware of where the big growth opportunities lie: Brazil, India, and China. They know that if they can come up with the right global brand ideas, they can hit these new markets faster and more effectively, without having to reinvent the wheel each time.

The challenge is in finding that "right idea." If it's based on some small quirk of the local culture, it may not travel. Commercials, especially humorous ones, are often based on a funny line or thought that may not translate well into another language or culture. Movement ideas, on the other hand, are more apt to tap into universal ideas about pursuing passions, expressing oneself, overcoming challenges, or getting things done. Even with all the real and sometimes significant cultural differences that do still exist, there are a lot of these underlying common threads that connect people across borders.

MOVEMENT ENVIRONMENTAL AWARENESS IN POOR COUNTRIES

EXEMPLAR GREEN BELT MOVEMENT INTERNATIONAL

THE BIG IDEA The Green Belt movement provides income and sustenance to millions of people in Kenya through the planting of trees. It also conducts educational campaigns to raise awareness about women's rights, civic empowerment, and the environment throughout Kenya and Africa.

STARTED The Green Belt Movement was founded by Wangari Maathai, based in Nairobi, Kenya, in 1977. She was the first African woman to win the Nobel Peace Prize.

HOW IT SPREAD Currently there are two divisions of the Green Belt Movement: Green Belt Movement Kenya (GBM Kenya) and Green Belt Movement International (GBMI). Both divisions spread their message through lectures, volunteer work, an Internet presence, and dedicated spokespeople. There was a lot of publicity in 2004 when its founder, Professor Wangari Maathai, won the Nobel Peace Prize for her efforts with the Green Belt Movement, and later published an autobiography called *Unbowed*.

WHERE IT STANDS NOW More than 40 million trees have been planted and more than 30,000 women have been trained in forestry, bee-keeping, food processing, and other trades.

QUOTE "No matter what problems we face, we can still protect the environment and think of future generations. The message for Africans is that the solutions to our problems lie within us. The work we have been doing with the Green Belt Movement is a local response to a local problem."—Wangari Maathai

WEBSITE GreenbeltMovement.org

The Mahindra "Rise" movement offers a good example of how a universally appealing idea can cross borders—although at the same time, we found that it did require certain adjustments and adaptations to make it relevant to each particular culture. Universally, the idea is about "rising to the challenges of today." In India, the movement is focused more on India's current rise as a global player and achieving its destiny of becoming a leader in modern society; the focus is very much on achieving "first world" status.

In countries such as the United States and much of Europe, the message is likely to be expressed, and perceived, quite differently. There, the "Rise" movement will be much more focused on reinvention and challenging the status quo. These are countries that have already risen to leadership positions in the past. Now the feeling is that the challenge of the moment requires rejuvenation. While the "Rise" message was trying to speak to the differing aspirations of people around the world, it was also aimed at motivating Mahindra's multinational workforce. The previous credo, "Indians being second to none," no longer seemed to fit a company with a presence in China, the United States, Europe, Africa, and Australia, and with a growing workforce in all those regions. "Rise" was almost as much about connecting with global employees as it was about connecting with global consumers.

THE STATE OF BRAND MOVEMENTS AROUND THE WORLD

As an agency that operates in four very distinct parts of the world—we started in Europe, set up our headquarters in the United States, and have since branched out globally—we have a pretty good perspective on how the movement marketing phenomenon is playing out in different areas of the world. From what we've seen, the same changes (whether technological, social, or cultural) that are fueling interest in movements in the United States are doing the same thing around the world. If anything, the momentum toward movements may be even stronger outside the United States.

MOVEMENT ## EDUCATING IMPOVERISHED GIRLS

EXEMPLAR A GIRL STORY

THE BIG IDEA A Girl Story combines technology, animation, and storytelling to dramatize the experience of underprivileged girls in

India for Western viewers. This interactive, donation-based YouTube series tells the ongoing story of a fictional girl named Tarla who yearns to go to school and overcome other challenges. Her opportunities (and the film series's next installment) are directly controlled by the monetary donations of viewers, which allow her to proceed. Donors monitor the girl's progression through her tweets, Facebook updates, and subsequent videos. All proceeds go to the Mahindra Foundation, a nonprofit organization that supports Project Nanhi Kali, providing educational opportunities for Indian girls.

STARTED   StrawberryFrog started A Girl Story for the Mahindra Foundation's Nanhi Kali nonprofit project in 2010.

HOW IT SPREAD   The popularity of the unique message of A Girl Story spread through YouTube social sharing, extensive media coverage, and word of social media mouth, especially on Facebook.

WHERE IT STANDS NOW   A Girl Story is an ongoing mission and continues to help young girls in India advance and prosper. It is part of an organization that has dedicated 10 years of support to education and has reached more than 58,000 girls in India.

QUOTE   "We created an interactive experience. Your actions online not only have immediate filmic consequences, but real life consequences as well." —Josh Greenspan, maker of the videos

WEBSITE   Agirlstory.org

In Brazil, for example, several successful brand movements have taken hold for various clients, including one for a company called Pritt. If you think movements can be built only around inspiring or glamorous products, let me point out that Pritt makes . . . *glue sticks*. Pritt invented them, in fact, and has led the category for years. But as competition recently heated up, particularly from new, lower-priced products made in China, the brand needed to strengthen its connection with three critical (but very different) audiences: children (who are big users of glue sticks), their mothers (who buy them), and schools (which have a great influence on purchasing by way of school supply lists). Trying to reach those three very different constituencies with ads would have been a tough challenge. But with a movement, there was the possibility of bringing all three groups together around a shared endeavor.

Part of what sparked our thinking on this was ethnographic research with parents, kids, and educators. We found that in Brazilian schools (and probably in schools in many other countries, too, I'd wager), a big concern among educators is trying to find ways to get parents more involved in their kids' education. The "idea on the rise" in this particular culture was that there needed to be more ways to bring parents, teachers, and schools together to raise and teach kids. We all felt that this could be a movement, and Pritt wanted to lead it.

So the company immediately looked for ways in which it could serve a movement of this kind. One of the first steps was to establish an arts workshop, done in partnership with the Museum of Art of São Paulo, bringing together kids, parents, and teachers for collaborative art sessions involving collages, paintings, and other media. It was a remarkable program, particularly for parents and kids, who had the experience of learning side by side and working on art projects together. The art pieces that were produced became the print ads we ran for Pritt (as I've noted previously, a successful movement can actually create marketing content for you).

We also created an online platform that extended the movement beyond the workshops; it included an online gallery of works created by parents, kids, and teachers working together. As we began to expand the movement, we developed nearly 200 workshops in shopping malls throughout Brazil. At these workshops, participants worked on craft projects, but they also did something more: they engaged in discussions about the importance of strengthening the bond between schools, parents, and students to improve child development. We gradually invited people to become ambassadors for the movement, and 300 people took us up on that. Those 300 people were able to spread the word of this movement to 30,000 others, mostly parents and teachers.

GETTING "LAZY MEN" TO SHAVE

If Brazil has been very welcoming of brand movements, so too has India. We've launched several of our own, but one that caught my eye recently we had nothing to do with. It was launched by Procter & Gamble India's Gillette brand under the amusing banner of "Women Against Lazy Stubble" (W.A.L.S.), and it has attempted to bring together like-minded women around the country who happen to think, "It is about time men made a little effort to shave." The movement even has a manifesto that includes these two points:

- "[If] men don't shave, we will not cooperate with them."
- "If men don't shave, they shouldn't expect women to groom themselves either."

The idea for the movement apparently came out of P&G research showing that 85 percent of women prefer men to be clean-shaven. The company hired a few Bollywood actresses to serve as spokespersons, and the product placement in the movement struck me as a tad heavy-handed (here's a quote from one of the actresses leading the W.A.L.S. movement: "If women can spend hours in an effort to look good, then why can't men spend a mere five minutes of their time to look civilized and groomed? Now that the comfort of Gillette Mach3 is affordable, what excuses are left for men?"), so I guess I'd have to categorize this as movement lite: a fun little cause combined with a touch of blatant advertising. It'll be interesting to see how this kind of approach works.

We're currently working on a movement based in the heart of the Middle East, for the Dubai-based airline Emirates; while I can't say much about it here, I mention it as just more evidence that marketing movements are turning up in all kinds of unexpected spots around the globe. Of course, Europe continues to be a hotbed of movement marketing. It's where the Dove "Real Beauty" campaign was first dreamed up (to be specific, in the United Kingdom), and it's where leading fashion retail brands such as Diesel, IKEA, and H&M have been launching great global movements for years and, more recently, Heineken has launched a new global initiative rallying people around the concept "Open Your World."

THE GOLD-MEDAL CHAMP OF
ALL GLOBAL MOVEMENTS

Of all the terrific global marketing movements out there, the one that I believe serves as perhaps the best model of all is one that we don't tend to associate with marketing movements at all: the Olympic Games. Obviously, it's an international sporting competition first and foremost, but it's also a movement—one that began with an idealistic vision of bringing about change in the world, and one that global brands have been aligning with for decades.

Baron Pierre de Coubertin of France founded the International Olympic Committee in 1894 with the lofty ambition of reducing military conflict through sport—the basic idea was to channel the competitive rivalries between countries away from the battlefield and onto the playing field. Through the years, the Olympics have used all the classic tools of a movement—the flag, the five-rings symbol, the pledge, the ideals ("higher, swifter, faster")—and a lot of the techniques of growing a movement, which have served to continually bring new countries into the competition. And starting as early as 1912, marketers began to jump on the bandwagon. At that time, 10 Swedish companies purchased the rights to sell memorabilia of the games, held in Stockholm. By 1920, the official program was so full of ads that it was hard to find anything about the games themselves.

By now of course, Olympic sponsorship is a huge business. At the 2008 games, the price tag for being a global sponsor averaged out at more than $70 million per company (and closer to $100 million for the official main sponsor, Lenovo). What draws marketers is the eyeballs of TV viewers, for sure, but also, I think, a chance to be associated with something that stands for high ideals and high standards of excellence. On a grand scale, the Olympics offers what smaller movements also provide for marketers—a chance to be part of something that has real meaning in people's lives.

And even with all the money pouring into the Olympics, it seems to me that the games have managed to keep commercialism from overwhelming the ideals of the movement. I talked to Timo Lumme, the marketing director of the IOC, about this, and he offered some keen insights for those of us who are interested in the relationship between marketing and movements.

First of all, Lumme makes it clear that the ideals that are at the core of the movement—the ones instilled by the founders more than a century ago—have been central to its enduring success and growth. "This original idea that the [Olympic] rings stand for more than sport is a powerful one that really took hold with people," Lumme says. Even as the Olympics faced adversity through the years—and they have had their share, from terrorist incidents to financial troubles—the games survived in part because "the adversity tended to make people rally even more around that core ideal."

Lumme describes the Olympics as "a very disparate movement," with the IOC at the center, surrounded by some 80 national Olympic committees. And who are the "true believers" at the core of the movement? "The athletes," Lumme says. "They are the key influencers that make everything happen." Lumme says the elite athletes who actually compete in the games form the center circle of the movement; casual athletes form the next circle in terms of passionate advocates; nonathletes are the outer circle, although even for them there may be passionate interest tied to feelings of national pride, international goodwill, and so on.

The relationship with sponsors is a complex one. At the actual games, their presence is limited (no commercial signage is allowed at the venue, in stark contrast to what you find at the typical pro sports stadium today). "You don't want pollution of the ideal by too many commercial connotations," Lumme says. But brands find lots of ways to get mileage out of their Olympic marketing partnerships, starting with ads but not ending there. Internally, a company's Olympic marketing program is "often used to galvanize the company, almost creating a mini-Olympics movement inside the company," Lumme says.

Then there is the relationship with the host countries, who compete furiously for the rights to the games and, once chosen, may go all out to create a huge national movement around the games, as China did in 2008: the country spent an estimated $42 billion to prepare for and host the games. As someone who's been a participant in the process of bidding to be an Olympic host city (I worked on Stockholm's bid in 2004), I found it fascinating to see the way countries try to align with the Olympic ideals while also trying to add something new to the movement. (Our plan was to create the first totally recyclable environment at the Olympics; we lost to Athens, which had history on its side.) Once a city and country win a bid, they are expected to lead their own national uprising in terms of rallying an entire country behind the cause of putting on the best event possible. The basics of the movement—the ideals and the rules of the game—stay the same, but each host country gets to inject its own culture and flavor into the move-ment (and boy, did China do a job of that!).

So a big part of the Olympics' success, then, is their ability to gen-erate movements-with-the-movement. In doing this, they rely on the host countries, they rely on business partners, and above all, they rely on their most influential advocates, the athletes. The overall movement has lots of partners, each with its own reasons for being passionate and invested in the cause, but all of them dedicated to keeping the flame burning strongly. Talk about "sustaining a move-ment, and taking it global"—it would be hard to find a better model.

In the next and final chapter, we'll look at where movements go from here. The answer is complex, but here's a one-word preview: everywhere.

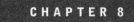

Why the Future Belongs to Movements

As mentioned in this book's preface, we're living in a time of uprisings. Maybe it's something in the air—a breeze that first started circulating during the Arab Spring and eventually found its way to Wall Street and beyond. More likely, what led to this global surge in movements was a confluence of forces, social and technological, creating a perfect storm that continues to rage. *New York Times* columnist Thomas Friedman put forth his own "grand theory" to explain it all: globalization and the info-tech revolution have made it easier for companies to downsize, putting more people out of work; governments, meanwhile, are cutting back on public assistance; income disparity between rich and poor keeps growing; and all the while, the same globalization/info-tech revolution that is fueling these changes is also enabling disenfranchised people to connect with one another and organize to take action. If you buy into Friedman's theory, this is not about one country's oppressive government or another country's corrupt leader; it's about a global phenomenon that is likely to keep spreading.

Watching all of this social upheaval on the news—let alone outside your window—can be unsettling, for sure. But there's a more positive way to look at this time of uprisings: all around the world, people who once might have suffered in silence are now making their presence felt. They're speaking out about long-festering problems and demanding fresh solutions.

In some cases, the people in the current wave of movements are doing more than asking for solutions—they're trying to help create them. Environmentalists, suddenly active again after a lull, are challenging the deniers head-on and pushing new approaches and strategies for sustainable living. A growing number of problem-solving groups, such as Charity: Water, are tackling massive challenges that involve getting water or food to the people in the world who need it most. Movements continue to spring up to save endangered species (including one that's close to my heart: "Save the Frogs!") or respond to the latest human crisis. In Japan, following the tsunami and the subsequent nuclear disaster, we witnessed the kind of courageous movement that is awe-inspiring: a group of Japanese pensioners came together to voluntarily put themselves in harm's way, taking the place of younger workers at the Fukushima power station.

MOVEMENT SENIOR POWER

EXEMPLAR   THE SKILLED VETERANS CORPS

THE BIG IDEA   The Skilled Veterans Corps is a group of retired senior citizens who stepped up to shoulder some of the burden of the cleanup in the aftermath of the earthquake and tsunami that devastated Japan. Primarily its members are volunteering to work at the stricken Fukushima Daiichi nuclear plant, replacing younger workers who would otherwise be exposed to dangerous radiation.

STARTED   Yasuteru Yamada founded the Skilled Veterans Corps in Tokyo in April 2011.

HOW IT SPREAD   Soon after the disaster struck, a core group of seniors, led by retired engineer and cancer survivor Yasuteru Yamada, age 72, began to reach out to 2,500 potential volunteers by phone and e-mail. Before long their plea had been repeated on Twitter and via blogs. Then the international news media went crazy over this elderly "suicide corps" (as it was called by the Japanese government, which was reluctant to accept its services), and within days the movement had received more than 900 donations and 250 able-bodied seniors offering their services.

WHERE IT STANDS NOW   The group's website outlines the steps the corps would take to help the nuclear plant. More than 500 volunteers are ready to help, but the government remains reluctant to put them into service.

QUOTE   "Those of us who hailed the slogan that 'Nuclear Power is Safe' should be the first to join. This is our duty to the next generation and the one thereafter. Senior people, elderly people, will get less influenced by radiation. Therefore, we say older people should take action."—Yasuteru Yamada

WEBSITE   Svcf.jp/english

What all of these movements have in common—from the political protests to the folks bringing water or trying to preserve the environment—is a willingness to face up to daunting challenges.

The members of these uprisings are, for the most part, ordinary people who've taken a stand, deciding that *somebody* has to do *something*—and that since our leaders aren't willing or able to solve these problems for us, we have to do it ourselves. But we can't do it alone; we need help from a few like-minded souls.

So while the rise in uprisings can seem ominous, it may also represent the first stirrings of a new era of progress. What it could mean is that the world's citizens have finally figured out that they need to get together and start trying to make things better.

Given that there is so much in the world that needs fixing, so many issues to be addressed, don't expect things to quiet down soon, says futurist Bob Johansen, who reports that everything points to a continuation of the growth in movements. His group, the Institute for the Future, foresees a world characterized by volatility, uncertainty, complexity, and ambiguity (VUCA). "It's not going to get better, and it will probably become worse," according to Johansen. And in the midst of the volatility, "movements will become increasingly important."

Johansen says people will respond to difficult times by seeking out groups, causes, and pursuits that can provide a sense of purpose, companionship, and meaning. Many of these will be constructive and creative (look for a big boom in movements that are about making things, or about joining together with others to build and fix things, says Johansen). But at the same time, he warns that we're likely to see "an increase in righteous movements that think everybody else is wrong."

Technology, of course, will continue to make it easier for people to link up and do things together. The popularity of Foursquare and other location-based networking technology is conditioning people to come together quickly and spontaneously. In most cases, they may be doing that just for fun on a night out, but the same capabilities that enable recreational "mass mingling" or playful flash mobs will also enable faster and more spontaneous movement gathering. As wireless data sharing gets faster and more powerful, it will make it continually easier to coordinate group actions in real time.

MOVEMENT OPEN INNOVATION NETWORKS

EXEMPLAR INNOCENTIVE

THE BIG IDEA Leveraging open innovation and crowdsourcing along with defined methodology, processes, and tools (such as cloud-based technology) can transform companies by helping them cost-effectively develop and implement solutions to their key problems, opportunities, and challenges.

STARTED Alpheus Bingham started InnoCentive in Massachusetts in 2001.

HOW IT SPREAD Key components in spreading interest were the successes of participants, word of mouth, and the Internet, which enables far-flung collaboration. Major companies such as Procter & Gamble, Dow AgroSciences, and Accenture put their challenges out in front of the public via InnoCentive and proved that actionable successes can come from this crowdsourcing.

WHERE IT STANDS NOW Today there are approximately 250,000 registered "solvers" from nearly 200 countries working through InnoCentive. More than $28 million in awards have been given to the solvers of the proposed problems. Large-scale companies participate, and there are multiple divisions (corporate, government, nonprofit, partners, and so on) that make up the business.

QUOTE "By unleashing human creativity, passion and diversity, we can solve problems that matter to business and society. Once you untether the search for solutions from an individual, department or company, amazing things happen." —InnoCentive.com, "What We Believe"

WEBSITE Innocentive.com

And if the tech guru Clay Shirky is correct, people also will have more time to pursue collective endeavors because of the "cognitive surplus": the leisure time that was once devoured by passively watching TV will increasingly be used for online activities that can connect us to kindred spirits and passionate interests. Shirky, like Johansen, sees a period ahead in which people will want to express themselves, make things, and find meaning. That will make them prime candidates for joining movements that may be tied to innovation, problem solving, or creative expression.

Then there is the social aspect. Because of technology, we're more connected than ever before—in one sense. But there's also a growing feeling that to some extent we may be trading "real" and substantial human relationships for the superficial virtual "friends" that pile up on Facebook. Movements can serve as an important new social hub; they can help bridge the real and the virtual worlds. Members of a movement may often initially connect online, but the action required by the movement can force people to come together and interact in the real world.

One last factor to consider is that the world is becoming increasingly inclined to help people start movements. There are ways to enlist financial support via crowdsourcing and online funding operations like Kickstarter (which is itself a movement, rallying people around the idea of pursuing worthwhile endeavors with help from the public). To assist with some of the tactical issues involved in starting and running a movement, there are informational and other support resources available from new groups such as Movements.org and Ark.com. In short, people increasingly will have the motivation, the time, and the means to start movements. But they still may need help in pulling it all together.

MOVEMENT ONLINE CROWDFUNDING

EXEMPLAR KICKSTARTER

THE BIG IDEA Kickstarter's purpose is to connect the power of social media to entrepreneurialism by providing an online gathering place where the public can fund artistic endeavors and individual projects can get off the ground. On Kickstarter, people pitch their creative projects (via video) and must meet predetermined benchmarks or no money changes hands.

STARTED Perry Chen, Yancey Strickler, and Charles Adler founded Kickstarter in April 2009.

HOW IT SPREAD From the beginning, the founders had a strong point of view about the kind of projects that would be featured on the site, so visitors could depend on quality control. The founders also made video pitching (with all the viral aspects of video sharing) a key feature of the project marketing. Extensive coverage via social media quickly followed, and, soon after, it was covered by the mainstream media. Creating the "curated pages" with a number of high-profile businesses and creative communities lent big-name power and credentials to the site.

WHERE IT STANDS NOW   At the two-year mark, more than 500,000 people had pledged more than $75 million to more than 11,000 start-up projects.

QUOTE   "Kickstarter is a way to work directly with your community and to build a little economy around your work—and make the thing you always wanted to make." —Yancey Strickler, cofounder

WEBSITE   Kickstarter.com

THE ROLE OF BUSINESS

So where does this leave business? Does it have a role to play? Some might suggest that it doesn't, and that business should steer clear of movements, for the sake of both movements and business. After all, movements often represent people's deep and passionate feelings about matters that may be of great importance to them; business could be seen as a corrupting force, introducing elements of insincerity, manipulation, and hype. From the standpoint of business, there are reasons to steer clear of movements, given that they can be unpredictable and volatile.

On the other hand, if the world is moving toward movements, how can business afford to be left behind? One of the biggest risks to business in today's dynamic world is being perceived to be out of touch and behind the times. If you represent the corporate establishment and are cut off from people's current needs and interests, you're as vulnerable as an entrenched and detached despot, ripe for overthrow. And while it's true that movement marketing requires a certain boldness on the part of companies, because it means that they must be willing to take more of a stand on some issues and give up trying to exert tight-fisted control of a brand and every expression of it, the reality is that companies and their brands probably no longer have the luxury of remaining overly cautious and timid. In a hyperconnected, ultra-competitive, and supercluttered marketplace, bolder actions and statements will be the only thing that will cut through and register with over-whelmed, marketing-weary consumers. Quite simply, to exist in this world, a brand has got to stand for something and prove it.

But what about the risk to movements from business? There are valid reasons for people to be skeptical about business and, in particular, about marketing. But at the same time, I think this lin-gering notion that business concerns and social issues don't mix is outdated; in today's world, the lines between business and social activities are blurring. Social entrepreneurs are bringing business savvy to the global problem-solving arena, while business leaders (such as Bill Gates) are helping to direct attention and resources to areas of need. Companies used to pay lip service to "corporate social responsibility," but today they are taking it much more seri-ously, knowing full well that they're being judged by consumers on everything from their environmental practices to their sup-port for diversity. The more business can be encouraged to be socially engaged and responsible, the better, because business has the kind of economic power and practical know-how that can play a huge role in taking on massive social challenges, empowering people to solve problems, or maybe just helping people to pursue a heartfelt passion. Aligning with movements provides a way for a "marketer" to behave more like a "contributor."

That may sound altruistic, but there are plenty of selfish reasons for business to support movements. It's in the interest of companies to deepen and strengthen their relationships with their customers by becoming more involved in their lives and the things they care about. Aligning with movements can also serve to clarify a company's purpose and mission and to strengthen its corporate culture. Being involved with movements can inject entrepreneurial energy into large, staid corporations. Dow just launched "Solutionism" and IBM has been very successful building a consistent movement around encouraging a "Smarter Planet." It can help challenger brands and start-ups gain a competitive foothold. From a purely self-interested, bottom-line-driven perspective, there are a lot of ways in which businesses can profit from their involvement with movements.

MUTUALLY BENEFICIAL SELF-INTEREST

And there's nothing to be ashamed of in that. In fact, what makes movement marketing interesting and appealing is that it does seem to offer the possibility of achieving a balance between selfless and selfish. It points the way toward a relationship between marketer and consumer that involves mutually beneficial self-interest. The same could not be said of traditional marketing and advertising, with the exception of the occasional pro bono ad. When marketers put efforts and resources into everything from rebuilding parks (Pepsi Refresh) to bringing together kids, parents, and teachers (Pritt), isn't that better than pouring those resources entirely into commercials?

The skeptics will probably be proven right about one thing, however: there will, undoubtedly, be some marketers who jump on the movements bandwagon and do more harm than good. Some may attempt to use a movement as simply a more covert form of advertising, injecting the worst elements of ads—the hype, insincerity, and one-way messaging—into their attempts to latch onto a popular idea or cause. Those ersatz movements will probably fizzle quickly; hopefully they won't discourage others, with bigger ambitions and better intentions, from taking a bold step.

I hope that instead, marketers will take a look at what brands like Pepsi, Nike and LIVESTRONG, Mahindra, Pritt, Smart Car, TOMS Shoes, and others mentioned in the preceding chapters have achieved. They might also want to look at the way Nissan has built a terrific movement around people who care passionately about zero-emission cars; it has been tremendously influential in the early success of the Nissan Leaf. Levi's has injected fresh energy into the old jeans brand with its highly inspirational and poetic "Go Forth" movement, aimed at rallying people around a new pioneer spirit.

And then there's a small start-up brand called PACT that has proved that you can build a movement around, of all things, underwear—though in this case it's underwear made from environmentally friendly materials. The brand's CEO, Jason Kibbey, says that he started the business as part of an attempt to "rethink consumption in a way that was more 'good' in the sense that you could consume with your values in place, and do the least possible harm to the environment. We had to figure out how we could use underwear as a platform for building awareness on critical issues." One of PACT's current movement initiatives involves partnering with the Sierra Club to protest the use of coal. "We just had 100 kids in our underwear protesting, and yeah, that gets attention," Kibbey says. "You have to connect your product with something that grabs attention to get your point across. However, we see it as more than a product—we're part of a larger collection of movements."

A VARIETY OF RELATIONSHIPS

In the days ahead, we'll see more instances of companies like PACT or TOMS Shoes, brands that are created with a movement philosophy in place from the outset. In these cases, the company really *is* the movement; the cause is indistinguishable from the business.

But the company-as-movement will be just one of several variations we can expect to see. There will be companies that launch new and original movements based around one of their existing brands. We'll see brands that form long-term partnerships with an outside movement (Nike and LIVESTRONG), but brands will sometimes form short-term relationships as well (AT&T did this by aligning itself with the TOMS Shoes movement for a time, while Google briefly championed the "It Gets Better" antibullying movement). Our client Mahindra has taken different approaches at different times. In the past, it has partnered with outside movements such as Nanhi Kali, an initiative aimed at educating girls in the developing world; more recently, with "Rise," the company created its own movement, which is now central to its culture and everything it does.

MOVEMENT SAFE WATER FOR THE WORLD

EXEMPLAR CHARITY: WATER

THE BIG IDEA The goal is to bring safe and clean drinking water and sanitation to the populations of developing nations by tapping into the easy-donation power of social media. After doing volunteer work in Africa, founder Scott Harrison set up his U.S.-based charity with a focused mission: to stop disease and death caused by polluted and untreated water across the world. Charity: Water partners with grassroots organizations that have already been set up in the communities. The business model is to give away 100 percent of public donations to projects. Videos of the projects' results are taken and shared.

STARTED   Scott Harrison founded Charity: Water in New York City in 2006.

HOW IT SPREAD   Harrison has a compelling personal reinvention story. That, along with huge fund-raising parties in Manhattan, garnered lots of media mentions. Social media is the main platform used to spread the mission and create collaboration among Charity: Water's "water partners." The charity gives partners a web page where they can recruit friends to donate with them, and it lets a partner post that page to Facebook and Twitter. Personal touches helped, too. Each $25,000 well gets a donor's name plaque on it. The charity recently added the Google Earth feature, which shows each well's location and enables information sharing about well building. The website features an animated video about "Why Water," with the narration of actress Kristin Bell, and offers many ways for people to do grassroots fund-raising.

WHERE IT STANDS NOW   The foundation has 25,000 "water partners" and has helped fund 3,962 projects in 19 countries, benefiting more than 1,795,000 people. In total, the organization has helped to raise more than $40 million as of July 2011. The 10-year plan is to raise $2 billion for clean water for 10 million people.

QUOTE   "Charity's a drag for many people. It's boring. It's bureaucratic. It's joyless. This is a blast. Knowing that we can give people clean water, going and meeting them. Seeing our donors' lives transformed." —Scott Harrison, founder

WEBSITE   Charitywater.org

Even as marketers find themselves aligning with movements in different ways and to varying degrees, it will be imperative that they conduct themselves with respect for the movements and with a certain amount of humility. Johansen makes the point: "Marketers need to recognize that they're starting in a deep hole, in terms of the fact that movement people may not want to listen to them or trust them. So they have to start by getting out of that hole. They need to be refreshingly honest. They need to recognize that they can't control social movements, but can offer resources to a movement—and hope the movement is willing to accept that offer."

On the subject of honesty, almost everyone agrees that it will be a critical factor in determining whether business can succeed in movement marketing. Today, people are "truth junkies." If you're not straight with them, they'll find you out and punish you for it. No one expects marketers involved in movements to be perfect, but they can't have a hidden agenda, and if they make a mistake, they'll have to be prepared to acknowledge it and fix it, instead of covering it up and spinning.

Anand Mahindra of the Mahindra Group told me that he thinks it's critical for companies to be honest with *themselves* as they're deciding on whether to get involved with a particular movement idea. "I do think a movement provides a fresh, differentiated way of approaching the market, but I also think if you're going to tap into a movement, you need authenticity," he says. "Either you're credible as a member or standard bearer of that movement, or you're not. Younger people will be the arbiters of this, and they can smell falsehood in a movement. So you have to choose carefully and say, 'Do I really belong to this movement?' And if you don't, you can't make genuflections to it, or change to try to conform to it."

WHAT ABOUT THE PRODUCT?

Does all this talk of honesty mean that movement marketing can never be caught in the position of trying to sell products? It's an interesting question. The Pepsi Refresh Project seems to have grappled with this; there were internal debates about how to link product promotion to the "Refresh" initiative. Should the movement be mentioned on cans, or tied to each purchase in some monetary way? Should people who buy Pepsi get movement perks, such as increased voting power in selecting projects? The former marketing director overseeing the initiative, Jill Beraud, noted that there was a delicate balance in trying to figure out how to boost sales without somehow tainting the movement as being overly commercial. Obviously, it's a balance that each marketer will have to work out, depending on its situation and its products. A company like Apple can talk about products all it wants, because people love those products so much. Other brands may have to take a softer approach.

To be sustainable, a brand movement probably will have to "sell" the product in some way, or at least show some tangible business benefit; in the results-driven world of commerce, programs that don't produce measurable results generally don't last long. But I think that on some level, even the people who are members of the movement get this; they understand that marketers are in business, and that there is some kind of trade-off involved. And I think if a company acts as a good, honest contributor and facilitator to the movement, then people will tolerate and even be interested in hearing about its product—*if* the company can find the right ways to work it into the conversation. To me, movement marketing has a hardware/software breakdown: the hardware is the product; the software is the ideals and ideas that drive the movement. In your messaging, you may be alternating back and forth, but it's better to err on the side of software.

THE GUIDING PRINCIPLE: "SHARE"

Another way to think about this is to be guided by the word *sharing*. Movement marketing is about *sharing* more than it's about *selling*. Again, this may sound hopelessly altruistic in a discussion about business, but it isn't really. Sharing can lead to selling, of course; marketers have long known that, which is the reason for free samples, introductory offers, and the like. But movement marketing opens up more possibilities for sharing, encompassing not just the product, but also, say, useful information that relates to the product (when parenting tips are shared on Pampers Village, the product benefits even if it isn't specifically mentioned in the discussion, by virtue of a halo effect on the company that's dispensing the useful info and advice). The key is to try to make sure that people actually want or need what you're sharing (if they don't, you're not sharing, you're foisting).

In the future of business, Johansen maintains, "Sharing and reciprocity will be the new currency." Or, as another futurist/innovation guru, Charles Leadbeater, puts it, in the new marketing landscape, "you are what you share." Technology will encourage more sharing between companies and customers. For example, Johansen points out that cloud computing offers greater ability to share resources in a systematic way. "In the cloud, the more you give away, the more value is created," he says.

Sharing goes two ways, however. With a brand movement, it's important to allow members of the movement to share what they have to offer, whether it's their time and energy, their ideas and stories, their feedback, or something else. Let them help you to create content, organize the movement, or engage with the brand through various forms of structured participation.

MOVEMENTS FOR ONE AND ALL

Movements are about masses of people, but they're also about the individuals within the group. Ultimately, to be most effective, brand movements of the future will be highly personalized, making people feel that the movement is speaking directly to their interests and aspirations. If you look at where technology is going, it's toward a world in which each of us can surround himself or herself with what most interests him or her. Through the use of algorithms and other customization tools, we'll be able to individualize movements based on customized interests and lifestyles, and thereby deliver a highly personalized experience. Movements might, for example, be broken down into life stages: I can envision the "Rise" movement offering one kind of experience for a college student and something quite different for an older person.

Meanwhile, in the days ahead, it will be interesting to watch as movements take off in all kinds of unexpected directions. Even as they're driven by technology, they'll help us to cope with the new technological world. We can expect online privacy movements to gain force, along with parallel movements fighting to keep the Internet free of regulation. Geek-and-gadget movements will be balanced by movements yearning for simplicity and low-tech activities (such as "made-by-hand" movements, which are already big and getting bigger). At the outer tech limits are movements such as Singularitarianism, which is based on the belief that one day computers and robots will outsmart humans—and if and when this superintelligence (called the Singularity) happens, the movement believes, we'd better be prepared.

MOVEMENT **TECHNOLOGY AND THE FUTURE OF MANKIND**

EXEMPLAR SINGULARITARIANISM

THE BIG IDEA The Singularitarianism social movement is based on the concept that one day computers and robots will outsmart humans. This is called the Singularity. The movement believes deliberate action needs to be taken now to ensure that, if and when superintelligence happens, the Singularity benefits human beings. One such idea is combining humans and machines to achieve a super race that will eliminate poor health and death.

STARTED Mark Potts founded Singularitarianism in 1991; it has recently been popularized by Ray Kurzweil.

HOW IT SPREAD Singularitarianism has had a foothold in techie and academic circles for years. Well-attended lectures, articles, meetings, and comparisons to a religious movement attest to the zeal of the movement. The Internet is also a huge venue for Singularity information sharing, led by the slick, trendy website SingularityHub.com.

WHERE IT STANDS NOW Members of the movement are launching Singularity University, based in Silicon Valley, to "assemble, educate, and inspire a cadre of leaders who strive to understand and facilitate the development of exponentially advancing technologies." Singularity U is supported by many big names in tech, such as Google, Autodesk, Nokia, and Cisco. Recent "Man vs. Machine" events such as *Jeopardy* pro Ken Jennings playing against—and losing to—an IBM supercomputer have thrust the notion of the Singularity into the mainstream, as evidenced by stories on the movement in *Time*, *USA Today*, and the *New York Times*.

QUOTE "We will transcend all of the limitations of our biology. That is what it means to be human—to extend who we are." —Ray Kurzweil

WEBSITE Singularityhub.com

The political realm has always had movements on the left and right, but look for a big rise in movements that lie somewhere in the middle. Mark McKinnon (interviewed in Chapter 5) has gotten things started with the "No Labels" movement, which is trying to find common ground between the polarized extremes of liberalism and conservatism. And in mid-2011, Starbucks chief Howard Schultz jumped into the fray, starting a movement called "Upward Spiral" that was born out of Schultz's frustration with the partisan bickering in Washington. Before taking his movement to the larger public, Schultz began by rallying the support of key influencers: he enlisted 100 business leaders who promised to withhold campaign contributions unless the government found ways to break the gridlock and take bipartisan action on pressing budget issues. Meanwhile, yet another new movement, "Americans Elect," was trying to create the first "direct nomination" of presidential candidates in the 2012 election. Unaffiliated with any political party or ideology, the initiative is seeking to use the Internet and an online convention in mid-2012 to give every single voter the chance to choose the candidates that will end up on the Americans Elect ballot in each state. The overriding theme in all of this is that people are concluding that the current political system no longer works—and that, through movements, it may be possible to fix or even replace that system.

In addition to taking on politics, technology, and various other issues, movements can be expected to take on business as well. Obviously, the OWS movement has targeted the financial industry. Meanwhile, in the United Kingdom, opening up a new supermarket isn't as easy as it used to be. The chain Tesco (among others) has seen plans for new stores blocked by neighborhood uprisings that have been exceedingly well organized and have drawn national attention. And if you're thinking of buying the local football club, and that club happens to be the beloved Manchester United team, be prepared for the team's fan-shareholders to have their say. The Manchester loyalists, reacting to plans by the majority owner (who first tried to sell the team to Rupert Murdoch, then subsequently announced plans to take money out of the club to pay down other debt), have staged a classic uprising, complete with dramatic symbolic gestures: The fans have taken to wearing bright green and gold scarves (celebrating the team's original colors) to show solidarity with one another.

Expect future movements to endeavor to keep marketers honest and products safe and reliable. They may occasionally use a brand's own ads against it: Greenpeace, angered by Volkswagen's opposition to new CO_2 emission standards, recently created an online movement that spoofed Volkswagen's popular Star Wars–themed commercial "The Force." Suggesting the VW had "turned to the dark side," the group set up a site, VWdarkside.com, that tried to rally people to join forces against the carmaker by signing petitions.

We'd better get comfortable with movements, because it seems there's no turning off the power that drives them. During the 2011 London riots, local authorities briefly entertained the fantasy that they could somehow calm things down by cutting off BlackBerry instant messaging service. The plan was never enacted, and it's probably a good thing it wasn't—because even as the riots were winding down, social media was critical in organizing a spontaneous movement to clean up the mess and repair the damage. Using Twitter and Facebook, the initiative tagged "Riot Cleanup" quickly drew 90,000 followers—who were instructed on how to participate in organized efforts to set things right again in London.

If there's a lesson there, it may be this: movements can make a mess of things, or they can build things up and make them better. But they're not going away, so we'd all better figure out which side we're on.

Notes

CHAPTER 1

Page 6: "In times of turbulence, anything that gives people a sense of meaning tends to grow." Bob Johansen was interviewed for this book by Warren Berger.

Page 11: "In his book *Tribes*, the author and marketing guru Seth Godin describes a movement as 'an idea that spreads with *passion* through a community.'" Seth Godin, *Tribes* (New York: Portfolio, 2008).

Page 18: "The author Clay Shirky has observed that this confluence." Clay Shirky, *Here Comes Everybody* (New York: Penguin Press, 2008).

Page 19: "The sociologist Neil Smelser has theorized that social movements come about because of a combination of factors, starting with social strain." Smelser's theories, which are referred to several times in the book, are explained in Diana Kendall, *Sociology in Our Times* (Belmont, CA: Thomson Wadsworth, 2005) and Donatella Della Porta and Mario Diani, *Social Movements: An Introduction* (Malden, MA: Blackwell Publishing, 2006).

Page 20: "And while it's generally understood that today, anyone who is using social media has 'three degrees of influence.'"

The three degrees of influence concept is covered in Nicholas Christakis and James Fowler, *Connected: The Surprising Power of Our Social Networks and How They Shape Our Lives* (New York: Little, Brown, 2009).

Page 24: "The importance of 'Quiet Transparency.'" This term was used by Johansen in our interview with him.

CHAPTER 2

Page 29: "In a way, 'Think Small' was Ginsberg's *Howl* from 1956 as an ad." Dominik Imseng's analysis of the Volkswagen ad is taken from his interview for this book by Warren Berger, and also from his book, *Think Small: The Story of the World's Greatest Ad* (Full Stop Press, 2011).

Page 29: "You could take an inverse delight in not having to keep up with the Joneses." Julian Koenig's quotes appear in Imseng's book as well as in the documentary film *Without Walls* by Joanna Mack.

Page 29: "The Volkswagen campaign was rich in the kind of semiotics." The discussion of Helmut Krone's design elements uses ideas from Imseng's book and Mack's film.

Page 34: "Apple 'enabled people to do things they couldn't do before.'" Guy Kawasaki was interviewed for this book by Warren Berger.

Page 35: "The psychologist Ross Goldstein studied Apple customers." Goldstein's research and quotes appeared in Leander Kahney, "Mac Loyalists: Don't Tread on Us," *Wired*, December 2002.

Page 40: "The *Adweek* columnist Barbara Lippert commented . . . that the Dove campaign 'goes against what everybody did for 50 years, which is make you anxious about how you look.'" Lippert said this as a guest on *The Early Show*, CBS, October 20, 2006.

SIDEBAR

Page 50: "As the Wii took off in the United Kingdom, some remarkable figures emerged: two-thirds of parents with kids aged 10 to 15 reported that it was encouraging their kids to exercise more." Research cited in Ian Williams, "Social Gaming Bringing Families Together," V3.co.uk, http://www.v3.co.uk/v3-uk/news/1993726/social-gaming-bringing-families.

CHAPTER 3

Page 58: "Mark Earls, who has studied the phenomenon of group behavior." Several of Earls's ideas cited in this chapter, including his term *we-species* and his discussion of the "wave," are from his book *Herd: How to Change Mass Behavior by Harnessing Our True Nature* (Hoboken, NJ: John Wiley & Sons, 2009).

Page 60: "People join these types of groups not to escape themselves, but rather, 'to become *more* themselves.'" Douglas Atkin's observations about why people join certain types of groups/cults, including brand movements, are taken from his book *The Culting of Brands* (New York: Portfolio, 2004).

Page 61: "A landmark study conducted 40 years ago by the psychologist Henri Tajfel." This study is well known and is quoted in many places, but for an interesting fresh take, see the post "Revealed: How Steve Jobs Turns Customers into Fanatics," on the blog "Neuromarketing: Where Brain Science and Marketing Meet," August 25, 2010, http://www.neurosciencemarketing .com/blog/articles/us-vs-them.htm.

Page 65: "The leaders of the growing Aging in Place movement." The founders of this movement were interviewed for this book by Laura O'Connor.

Page 69: "Ned Dodington, who along with Matthew Wettergreen has launched Caroline Collective." The founders of this movement were interviewed for this book by Laura O'Connor.

Page 72: "'People want to make a contribution.'" Daniel Pink's comments were taken from an e-mail interview for this book conducted by Scott Goodson.

Page 73: "What the writer Clay Shirky refers to as a 'shared endeavor.'" Shirky uses this term both in *Here Comes Everybody* (New York: Penguin Press, 2008) and in his next book, *Cognitive Surplus* (New York: Penguin Press, 2011).

Page 74: "Angela Daffon started a movement called Jodi's Voice." Daffon was interviewed for this book by Laura O'Connor.

SIDEBAR

Page 78: Faythe Levine was interviewed for this book by Laura O'Connor.

CHAPTER 4

Page 83: "Advice to the youth of Egypt: Put vinegar or onion under your scarf for tear gas." From David Kirkpatrick and David E. Sanger, "A Tunisian-Egyptian Link That Shook Arab History," *New York Times*, February 14, 2011.

Page 85: "The public square; . . . where, as author Steven Pinker has noted, private knowledge would become public knowledge." Pinker's views on why revolutions tend to start in the public square are explained in his presentation "Language as a Window into Human Nature," http://fora.tv/2011/02/04/ Steven_Pinker_Language_as_a_Window_into_Human_Nature.

Page 86: "Technology has opened up new—and more—options for creating a movement and engaging in one." Dr. Kathleen Gerson was interviewed for this book by Laura O'Connor.

Page 87: "The sociologist Saskia Sassen of Columbia University observes." Dr. Sassen was interviewed for this book by Laura O'Connor.

Page 88: "Movements.org . . . provides 'a support network for grassroots activists.'" Jason Liebman's quote appears on the Movements.org website.

Page 88: "Purpose.com is 'attempting to deploy the collective power of millions of citizens.'" The group's founder, Jeremy Heimans, was interviewed for this book by Laura O'Connor.

Page 89: "*Wired* magazine recently declared that the rise of social media represents 'the vanguard of a larger cultural movement.'" From Kevin Kelly, "The New Socialism," *Wired*, June 2009.

Page 93: "Scientists who study 'swarm intelligence' have found that the group is able to share information instantly." Among the many articles on swarm intelligence, two of the best are Peter Miller, "Swarm Theory," *National Geographic*, July 2007, and Carl Zimmer, "From Ants to People, an Instinct to Swarm," *New York Times*, November 13, 2007.

Page 99: "One of the brand movements of the past few years that I really admire is TOMS Shoes." The full story of the TOMS movement is told in Blake Mycoskie, *Start Something That Matters* (New York: Spiegel & Grau, 2011).

Page 102: "'We're forecasting a permanently VUCA world.'" Bob Johansen of Institute for the Future was interviewed for this book by Warren Berger.

Page 102: "John Bielenberg, who has launched a number of grassroots movements." Bielenberg was interviewed by Warren Berger. His quote about students moving beyond just wanting a Saab originally appeared in Warren Berger, *Glimmer* (New York: Penguin Press, 2009).

Page 106: "We're moving toward an inflection point." Marc Pritchard's quote is from Rajiv Banerjee, "The World Is Heading Toward Marketing 3.0," *Economic Times*, July 7, 2010.

Page 106: "The values revolution is being amplified by the digital revolution." Sebastian Buck is quoted in Andrew Adam Newman, "Good/Corps Aims to Help Business Meet Social Goals," *New York Times*, May 13, 2011. (The same article quotes the Edelman study showing that 87% of Americans believe companies should be concerned with societal interests.)

SIDEBAR

Page 108: Former Pepsi marketing director Jill Beraud was interviewed for this book by Warren Berger.

CHAPTER 5

Page 121: "A great example of this is Dan Savage's remarkably successful 'It Gets Better' movement." Information about the origin of this movement, as well as the quote from Savage, is taken from the website www.itgetsbetter.org.

Page 127: "Mass movements can rise and spread without belief in God—but never without belief in a devil." From Eric Hoffer's definitive 1951 book on mass movements, *The True Believer* (New York: Harper & Row, 1951; New York: HarperCollins paperback, 1989).

Page 132: "As the *Washington Post* and others noted . . . , KFC produces food that could conceivably be seen as contributing to health problems." The *Washington Post* was one of many critics of this campaign; Jennifer LaRue Huget, "Is Buying KFC by the Bucket a Good Way to Fight Breast Cancer?," May 2, 2010.

Page 133: "The idea of 'Bold Choice' was really 'born out of the DNA of this brand.'" Kevin George of Jim Beam was interviewed for this book by Warren Berger.

SIDEBARS

Page 139: The interview with Erik Proulx was conducted by Laura O'Connor.

Page 141: The interview with political consultant Mark McKinnon was conducted by Warren Berger.

CHAPTER 6

Page 146: "But a lesser-known part of the story is that Apple built its movements . . . by starting from within." Lee Clow was interviewed for this book by Warren Berger. That interview is also the basis for the sidebar featuring Clow.

Page 148: "It's articulated in the writing of business gurus like Dov Seidman." Seidman's philosophy on the importance of how business conducts itself is laid out in his book *How: Why How We Do Anything Means Everything* (Hoboken, NJ: Wiley, 2011).

Page 156: "A great example . . . was a campaign/movement started a few years ago by the Pedigree pet food brand." Details of the Pedigree story come from Berger's interview with Clow; this campaign also is chronicled in Warren Berger, Jean-Marie Dru, and Lee Clow, *Disruption Stories* (New York: TBWA, 2005).

Page 162: "In a recent campaign for Sharpie markers, created by the brand and its agency, Draftfcb." The campaign is described in Jane Levere, "A Sharpie Campaign, Aimed at Teenagers, Urges Self-Expression," *New York Times*, July 26, 2011.

Page 163: "The swarm is always on the lookout for threats and opportunities." See the note on swarm intelligence articles in Chapter 4.

Page 165: "Douglas Atkin . . . observes that one of the chief ways in which brands can 'attract followers who will spread your brand gospel.'" From Douglas Atkin, "In Building Communities, Marketers Can Learn from Cults," *Forbes.com*, February 21, 2010.

Page 170: "A case in point is a small movie theater chain based in Austin, Texas." From Andrew Adam Newman, "In Cellphone Wars, Movie Chain Uses a Violator's Words," *New York Times*, June 23, 2011.

Page 174: "Any movement has to have its own unique symbols and flags." Collins's quote originally appeared in Warren Berger, *Glimmer* (New York: Penguin Press, 2009).

Page 174: "It's hard to think of any that made better use of such symbolism than LIVESTRONG." Information on the LIVESTRONG campaign comes from Warren Berger's interview for this book of Marty Cooke (who is also featured in a sidebar).

Page 176: "Comedian Ben Stiller has had some playful fun with LIVESTRONG and the yellow wristbands." See Stiller's YouTube video, which can be found at the site www.Stillerstrong.com.

CHAPTER 7

Page 184: "Suddenly, the *New York Times* was writing about 'Scion Speak.'" From Lynnley Browning, "Do-It-Yourself Logos for Proud Scion Owners," *New York Times*, March 24, 2008.

Page 189: "The marketer and blogger Gareth Kay notes that in today's media environment, 'The bigger a brand gets, the smaller it must act.'" Quotes from Gareth Kay's May 13, 2011,

post on his excellent "Brand New" blog, http://garethkay
.typepad.com/brand_new/2011/05/think-small.htm.

Page 190: "Sharpie . . . sees its role as a *curator.*" Atkin quotes
about Sharpie from Douglas Atkin, "In Building Communities,
Marketers Can Learn from Cults," *Forbes.com*, February 21,
2010.

Page 193: Protesters in Syria acted "without organization,
strategy, or leadership." From Liz Sly, "Syrian Revolt Still
Spontaneous and Leaderless," *Washington Post*, July 28, 2011.

Page 193: "This type of movement is described as SPIN, or
'segmentary, polycentric, and integrated networks.'" From
Steve Breyman, "SPINning Syrian Protests," OpEdNews.com,
August 4, 2011.

Page 194: "The Obama campaign, in particular, understood
that by dispersing responsibilities widely." The Obama campaign's decentralized grassroots approach has been widely
covered, but particularly in Karen Tumulty, "How Obama Did
It," *Time*, June 5, 2008.

Page 195: "Scott Heiferman, the cofounder of Meetup, advises
that in order to use technology to harness the collective power
of communities." Heiferman addressed these points in his
presentation, "How to Spark a Movement in the Twenty-First
Century," South by Southwest, 2010.

Page 198: "A few years back, Unilever found itself dealing with
complaints." This criticism appeared in various media outlets, including Alana Semuels, "Group Has Axe to Grind with
Unilever," *Los Angeles Times*, October 10, 2007.

Page 201: "Before it was more of a global coordination as opposed to global management." Massimo F. d'Amore quote comes from Natalie Zmuda, "Pepsi Beverage Guru Unveils His Plan to Win the World Over," *Advertising Age*, July 11, 2011.

Page 208: "It was launched by Procter & Gamble India's Gillette brand under the amusing banner of 'Women Against Lazy Stubble.'" From press release headlined, "Women Against the Lazy Stubble," on the Gillette-sponsored website www.shaveindia.com.

Page 209: "The Olympic Games . . . [is] a movement . . . that began with an idealistic vision of bringing about change in the world." Taken from Scott Goodson's interview of Olympics marketing director Timo Lumme, with timeline information taken from the USOC website.

CHAPTER 8

Page 213: "*New York Times* columnist Thomas Friedman put forth his own 'grand theory.'" From Thomas Friedman, "A Theory of Everything (Sort Of)," *New York Times*, August 13, 2011.

Page 218: "People also will have more time to pursue collective endeavors because of the 'cognitive surplus.'" See Clay Shirky, *Cognitive Surplus* (New York: Penguin Press, 2011).

Page 223: "And then there's a small start-up brand called PACT." Laura O'Connor interviewed PACT's CEO, Jason Kibbey.

Page 226: "I do think a movement provides a fresh, differentiated way of approaching the market, but I also think . . . you need authenticity." Anand Mahindra was interviewed for this book by Warren Berger.

Page 229: "As . . . Charles Leadbeater puts it, . . . 'you are what you share.'" That line is actually the title of the first chapter of Charles Leadbeater, *We-Think* (London: Profile Books, 2009).

Page 231: "In mid-2011, Starbucks chief Howard Schultz jumped into the fray." Schultz announced his new movement with a full-page ad in the September 4, 2011, *New York Times*, under the headline: "A letter to concerned Americans from Howard Schultz, CEO of Starbucks Coffee Company."

Page 232: "In the United Kingdom, opening up a new supermarket isn't as easy as it used to be." The uprising against Tesco and other supermarket chains is covered in John Harris, "Supermarket Sweep," *Guardian*, August 5, 2011.

Page 232: "The Manchester loyalists, reacting to plans by the majority owner." Information on the "green and gold" movement organized by the fans of Manchester United was provided by one of the movement's organizers, Duncan Drasdo.

Page 233: "Greenpeace, angered by Volkswagen's opposition to new CO_2 emission standards." The Greenpeace ad parodying Volkswagen's commercial can be seen on YouTube at www.youtube.com/watch?v=nXndQuvOacU.

Index